# UNCLE SAM'S BRIDES

## The World of Military Wives

# UNCLE SAM'S BRIDES

## THE WORLD OF MILITARY WIVES

*Bonnie Domrose Stone*
*and*
*Betty Sowers Alt*

## WALKER AND COMPANY

### NEW YORK

First published in the United States of America in 1990
by Walker Publishing Company, Inc.

Published simultaneously in Canada by Thomas Allen & Son
Canada, Limited, Markham, Ontario

Library of Congress Cataloging-in-Publication Data

Stone, Bonnie Domrose
Uncle Sam's Brides : the world of military wives / Bonnie Domrose Stone and Betty
Sowers Alt.
ISBN 0-8027-1099-9
1. Military wives—United States. 2. United States—Armed Forces—
Military life. I. Alt, Betty Sowers. II. Title.
U766.S76  1990      355.1′0973—dc20      89-39153

Printed in the United States of America

2  4  6  8  10  9  7  5  3  1

Of the many people who helped us with UNCLE SAM'S BRIDES, none deserve our heartfelt thanks more than our families. A special thanks to Leighton F., Doug, Greg and Paul Stone as well as Colonel Bill and Captain Eden Jeanette.

A special thanks to a dear friend, Helen Trent.

All the military wives who told us *write our stories* made UNCLE SAM'S BRIDES a reality. So many women agreed to be interviewed only if the authors would guarantee anonymity. To protect their husbands' careers, first names only have been used. These women are our heroines of today. Thank you.

# Contents

# Ranks

## ARMY/AIR FORCE/MARINES          NAVY/COAST GUARD

| | ARMY/AIR FORCE/MARINES | NAVY/COAST GUARD |
|---|---|---|
| 10 | General | Admiral |
| 09 | Lieutenant General | Vice Admiral |
| 08 | Major General | Rear Admiral |
| 07 | Brigadier General | Commodore |
| 06 | Colonel | Captain |
| 05 | Lieutenant Colonel | Commander |
| 04 | Major | Lieutenant Commander |
| 03 | Captain | Lieutenant |
| 02 | 1st Lieutenant | Lieutenant J. G. (Junior Grade) |
| 01 | 2nd Lieutenant | Ensign |
| | Chief Warrant Officer | |
| | Warrant Officer | |
| E-9 | Sergeant Major | Master Chief |
| E-8 | Master Sergeant | Senior Chief |
| E-7 | Sergeant 1st Class | Chief |
| E-6 | Staff Sergeant | 1st Class Petty Officer |
| E-5 | Sergeant | 2nd Class Petty Officer |
| E-4 | Corporal | 3rd Class Petty Officer |
| E-3 | Private First Class | Seaman |
| E-2 | Private 2 | Seaman Apprentice |
| E-1 | Private 1 | Seaman Recruit |

# UNCLE SAM'S BRIDES

## THE WORLD OF MILITARY WIVES

"An Army post is something like a company town . . . [giving the wife] far more opportunity, and probably more obligation, to help her husband in his career than most wives find in civilian life. . . . The people the wife meets at night, at parties, or in her home are the people her husband works for . . . protocol requires that the wife get to know the commanding officer and General's Lady."

—MRS. MARK CLARK
*Captain's Bride, General's Lady*

★ ★ ★

T raffic approaching the military base gate crawls to a halt as the gun-toting marine checks each car for a base sticker and each driver for a military I.D. card. Those without proper identification the marine waves off to one side. The experience is similar to border crossing—only this border separates the military from the civilians. Even though they are on United States soil, the barbed-wire fence and security force barricade an enclave totally dominated by the military. For here, as in thousands of other bases throughout the world, is a walled city, secured by its own military police and its own set of rules and governed by a separate military justice system.

As a "city" it contains an almost medieval closed society with its own clubs, tribal rituals, and language. It is a powerful nation closed to outsiders, controlled by its own set of laws, culture, rites of passage, and traditions. The passport for a wife to be admitted on base is her military I.D. card labeling her a D/W (dependent wife)—a card she must show to gain access to the military commissary, exchange, hospital, or recreational facilities.

While each base differs in its mission, most have the same functional buildings, warehouses, and war machines interspersed with family quarters. Most bases are complete in themselves, each equipped with a commissary, post exchange, chapel complex, hospital/clinic, library, family service center, recreation center, base theater, bowling alley, pool, and military club with membership restricted to respective ranks. A military wife need not ever venture off base.

Life seems so normal. There are marriages and children, visits to

★                              ★                              ★

the pediatrician, ballet lessons, Little League, schools, churches, and houses. There are centuries-old military traditions that have helped to shape colorful formal dinners, weddings, and promotions ceremonies.

There is no place on earth these women have not been. Madagascar, Istanbul, the islands of the Pacific. The great Northwest. Alaska. Puerto Rico. Germany. For more than two hundred years their eyes have seen columns of dust kicked up by hundreds of thousands of men marching across the globe. Following their warriors, these hardy women have made homes wherever the armies traveled.

No longer do these brides of Uncle Sam shelter beneath the canvas of wagons or in the bowels of troop ships plowing the Atlantic. No longer do they pass their days in rabbit warrens hacked out of the frozen plains of North Dakota. No longer do they fire their husbands' cannons or march down the same dusty roads traveled by weary caissons.

Times have changed; time has stood still. Although each base, each city of Uncle Sam's, has all the modern conveniences, it is constructed along the same lines of demarcation seen in early forts. In spite of ordinary appearances, no one ever forgets that this city is totally commanded and dominated by the military. The homogeneous population is carefully preserved. Undesirables are culled; unpromotables are dumped; internal rules and regulations are tightened to keep only what the military considers the best and brightest.

When a woman marries a military man she moves into his world and is pressured to conform and perform as a "good" military wife. She is literally brainwashed by peer pressure, lectures she is "requested" to attend, and military literature. There are books that set out correct manners and performance expected of a military wife. Magazines, specifically published for military wives and distributed free at commissaries and exchanges, tell her how to dress, perform socially, cook gourmet meals, how to cope with loneliness, how to survive a move, how to shop economically, how to decorate a tempo-

&#42;      &#42;      &#42;

rary home. At wives' coffees, older wives tell new wives exactly what is expected of them. The pressure is more intense on a young officer's bride. She is told she can make or break her husband's career. Her family will be in fierce competition to be *the* model family, without blemishes, always earning the best grades, attending the best schools, always doing what is expected—for to do less would tarnish the husband's reputation. Actually, the pressure on an officer's wife never lets up, even after her husband is promoted. If, for example, he is to have a command, he attends command school while she attends classes for commanders' wives that outline her new duties.

With her marriage, her whole life will be consumed by the military. While a civilian mother may prohibit her children from playing with G.I. Joe paraphernalia because it is too warlike, the military wife brings up her children near a live ammunition storage dump, with ponderous tanks thundering past her window, or warships tied up in the harbor just down the street from where she lives. She raises her children to the sounds of troops marching in cadence, cannons booming at sunset, a recorded bugle call summoning troops to sunrise formation, the window-rattling whine of jet engines clearing the runway on a flight path over her quarters. For prolonged periods of time she rears her children in the strained atmosphere of a single-parent home, near nests of other single parents—for Daddy always seems to be playing at war games.

To play war games, each service has its own set of uniforms that distinguishes it from the others. Insignias mark the achievements of the Top Guns or Green Berets or Fighter Squadron or Submarine Force. The submariner wears a dolphin pin above his left breast pocket; wings designate a pilot. Patches on a flight suit distinguish members of Military Airlift Command from Strategic Air Command or Tactical Air Command. The Army Airborne Rangers earn their vivid patch by completing a grueling survival course. Beribboned uniforms tell at a glance what honors each has earned. The uniform makes the man, it is said. The stripe of gold on a hat or the silver of

**5**

★          ★          ★

an eagle on a shoulder board marks an officer as someone to be obeyed. The stripes of the enlisted designate someone who can be ordered about—and always is.

It is not just the men who are marked. Wives assume social "rankings" based on their husbands' ranks and jobs. An academy graduate is at the top of the heap. His wife will undoubtedly be a "ring knocker," wearing her engagement diamond set into his academy ring so there will be no mistaking her social status. Wives also take on the distinctive coloration of their husbands' jobs. Wives of flyers or submariners wear miniatures of their husbands' wings or dolphins pinned onto their collars. All of these accoutrements can be important to the wife who views herself as somewhat separate from and certainly above those with whom she is socializing.

Wives are known to wear their husbands' rank. While not actually holding any military rank themselves, and, indeed, totally dependent on their husbands for their place in the military, wives often identify themselves with their husbands' rank so that others may correctly place them in the military hierarchy. "Hello, I'm Pat Smith, wife of Colonel Smith," as she checks into the dispensary, alerts the medical staff to her position of power. Wives drive cars marked with the ranks of their husbands. An officer's insignia on a car is saluted coming on base—even if the wife is driving. If the car has an 0-6 (senior officer) insignia, the wife can take advantage of preferential parking at the base commissary, club, or exchange. "Senior" wives also have the privilege of sitting at the head of the table or being honorary chair of base functions.

While her husband is celebrating his manhood in a series of war games designed to keep the armed forces at fighting strength, the military officer's wife is expected to play the part of dress-up Barbie to his G.I. Joe. In the unique setting of a military base the officer's wife is molded into a "good" military wife and is expected to sublimate her life to his career, to fit into a secondary role in which her aplomb as a hostess or ability to dress well and entertain are primarily

★               ★               ★

the ways in which she is judged by her peer group—the other officers' wives. As one general told a group of colonels' wives, "You are on display twenty-four hours a day and are models for the lower ranks. You must always be aware of what you say, what you do, and how you dress."

There are no such expectations for the enlisted wife, as will be explained in Chapter 2. However, all wives have access to "acceptable" preoccupations that revolve around base activities. They can play golf or tennis, bowl, take art or ceramic lessons, or give countless hours to the Red Cross or base thrift shop. They can perform all their duties quite separate from the civilians and all within the confines of one of Uncle Sam's company towns.

This separation mentality of *us* (the military) versus *them* (the outside world) may have formed in the days of armed forts and Indian rampages, but it continues to dominate the lives of today's military families. Many military wives, even in the United States, said they rarely go "off base"—as though they were still living deep in enemy territory while on American soil. There is such comfort in being surrounded by the military that many wives interviewed said they preferred the "safety" of living on base, especially if their husbands were in a sea-going command or were often deployed. This sense of "us versus them" is even more pronounced overseas, where wives tend to retreat to the home base, restricting activities to the compound and generating a frenetic local scene within their own group of Americans.

Even though today's military "cities" may lack the unbridled luxury that military officers' wives enjoyed overseas prior to World War II, the retirees know that the best the country can offer is found on these bases—with rank, of course, enjoying the most privileges.

## THE COMPANY TOWN

Uncle Sam runs a company town, a company whose sole business is war. From the moment a woman marries a military man and moves onto a base (and often the military orders families to live on base when housing is available), she leaves behind most of her civilian status. She may have been a college professor, a student, an employee of a Fortune 500 company, a nurse, yet from the military standpoint she is viewed only as the "dependent wife" of the military man, with her status (or lack of it) totally based on his standing in the military.

The military wife strives to maintain a normal home life while raising children in a military environment. Her pioneering is done not in a covered wagon but in a station wagon brimming with children and belongings as she travels—often alone—from one military base to another. In military quarters, she opens doors on rooms filled with the ghosts of those who have played and loved and cried, then—tour of duty over—packed and moved on. Our heroines are these women who each day quiet aching hearts as they prepare their fatherless children for one more day of living, while Daddy plies his trade around the world. How do you honor the heroism of these valiant women? Each morning, as the sun sweeps across the globe, the ordinariness of their lives is fully illuminated. Alone, they have babies and nurse infants; sweep and clean and teach. They create a patchwork of many jobs, of many starts and stops of a career, of children housed and educated all over the globe.

The man the military wife sends off to work in the morning is not employed in an innocuous trade. He is not a clerk in a store. He is a warrior, a trained killer always on alert and ready to move out on a moment's notice. Each day military wives fight the terror of the unseen enemy, knowing their men may never come home again. The courage sewn into the pattern of their lives is not the courage of the battlefield. Most wives do not risk life and limb as do their husbands. But they do embody compassion, courage, and the conviction of knowing their value in keeping peace on the planet. For each woman who completes a military career by her husband's side does so with the strong conviction that serving in the military is more than a job; it is a commitment to keep the nation strong and the gossamer threads of peace intact.

★       ★       ★

As will be seen in Chapter 3, a military wife is often alone. Rarely will her husband have a nine-to-five job. Even if he works a desk job, you can bet he also "stands the duty" away from home at his military post for as long as twenty-four hours straight. He may be deployed in a submarine for nearly a year or out in the field for a couple of months. The military wife may end up living in a nearly all-female compound if most of the men are deployed at the same time.

Military personnel receive a "housing allowance," which is an assessed amount determined by each service member's rank (see Appendix). The higher the rank the higher the allowance. If the service member lives in base housing the allowance is deducted from his or her pay. If the service member rents or buys in a civilian community he receives the housing allowance in his pay voucher. This may be augmented by COLA (cost-of-living allowance) to offset the higher cost of living in areas such as Washington, D.C. For example, in 1989, an E-7 (senior enlisted)* without dependents who was stationed in Ketchikan, Alaska, would receive an additional $334.02 in Variable Housing Allowance (VHA) to help offset the higher cost of living. That same E-7 would receive no additional monies if stationed at either Fort McClellan or Fort Ruker, Alabama. An officer (O-3) would receive slightly more VHA. His monthly housing increase would be $398.19 for the same base in Alaska. At any time the VHA could be eliminated. Also, say some, it barely helps compensate for the true cost of living in the more expensive cities.

John Ginvosky reported that in trying to make ends meet, more military families are resorting to using food stamps. The Air Force Commissary Service noted that in fiscal 1987, Air Force families redeemed "a little more than $3 million worth of food stamps." In 1988 the figure rose to $3.4 million. In just the first quarter of 1989, "Air Force shoppers redeemed $1 million worth of food stamps."

*For clarification of officer and enlisted ranks, see chart.

Army family members were reported to have redeemed $5.2 million worth of food stamps in 1988; the Navy $2 million, and the Marines about $400,000. No explanation was given as to the reason for the differences between the services in food stamp usage.

Not all military families live on base. There are not enough government quarters to house the married troops. (The Air Force, for example, estimates that two-thirds of its families live off base with 112,000 housed on bases.) As in any large organization, newcomers receive the lowest salary and fewest "perks." For those E-4 and below in rank—the very people who can least afford to live off base—the military does not authorize housing. They are eligible for base quarters only if a surplus of units is available.

An E-4's housing allowance in 1987 was $188.40 per month without dependents. With dependents he received a total of $275.40 to house them. Depending on his years in service, that same E-4 could take home anywhere from $814 to $1,019 per month. By 1989, modest raises brought an E-4's monthly basic pay up to $912.60 (with two years of service.) His basic allowance for quarters, with dependents, rose to $303.60. In 1989, an 0-10 could be taking home $6,291.60 per month. He would pay only $754.50 monthly for his government quarters. The senior officer has more disposable income for housing should he be quartered in the civilian sector. More than likely, he will be living on base in the best the military has to offer, while the young E-4 is calling a run-down minuscule apartment home, for he is rarely eligible for military housing. Says John Burlage, writing in the *Air Force Times*, if you include what the military calls the regular military compensation, which is all inclusive of basic pay, subsistence allowance, basic allowance for quarters and average variable housing allowance, in 1989 that same E-4 is said to have earned $17,462 annually. The regular military compensation for an 0-10, if he had served for 18 years, would be $94,411 anually.

The military wife takes what the housing office assigns to her husband on a first-come, first-served basis, depending on what unit is

★                              ★                              ★

available in the area for her family size and—most importantly—her husband's rank. She cannot choose her neighbors or her neighborhood.

The civilian world crawls toward the time when segregation by virtue of race or religion will no longer exist; the military eliminated this segregation with one blow in the form of a mandate. However, segregation among the ranks is still operating both on and off duty based on a long-established doctrine in the military culture of nonfraternization. The military's concept is that rigid discipline is essential to success in battle and fewer casualties on the battlefield. Having the lower ranks socially mingling with the higher ranks weakens discipline and threatens the military mission. The military spouse is a victim of this concept and is segregated—as she has been for the last two hundred years—either in enlisted quarters on "Soap Suds Row" or in Officer Country. At times, the line of demarcation is so sharp—a canal, a fence, a broad expanse of grass—that military wife and author Ann Combs has written, "They might as well run barbed wire down the middle of the street." There is even segregation within the ranks. The Navy has chiefs' housing for those E-7, E-8, and E-9 in rank. In the officer ranks, lieutenants and captains are housed in smaller quarters, quite different from major and lieutenant colonel housing. In most cases, housing for colonels/Navy captains is top of the line, surpassed only by the general's quarters.

This line of demarcation is strongly reinforced in the way housing is designed. The man with the most power on base—the general or admiral—has the largest house with the greatest expanse of lawn. Clustered around him will be officer housing, diminishing in size to the much smaller quarters assigned to junior officers. Depending on the size of the base (and on small or remote bases the ranks might be mixed), the enlisted are housed quite separate from officers. If it is available, the more senior enlisted have the better housing, whether it be eight-plex "townhouses," duplexes, or single-family dwellings. Sometimes the difference between officer and enlisted housing is less

**11**

*          *          *

perceptible; on other bases the grandeur of stately turn-of-the-century mansions reserved for senior officers can't be missed.

In military society—especially if she lives on base—a wife must socialize within the boundaries of a rigid caste system, rubbing elbows only with those of "her" rank. If an enlisted wife strikes up a friendship with an officer's wife she may be labeled as a brass polisher. The officer's wife will undoubtedly be taken aside and told, "We don't fraternize with the enlisted." In 1987, one Air Force officer's wife said "I never met an enlisted wife. They didn't live by us, they didn't attend the same club. I'd see them drinking beer at the bowling alley and think, 'Yuck!' I'm sure they thought we were stuck up."

## UNCLE SAM: THE NATION'S LARGEST MOVER

Each fiscal year, tens of thousands of military men and their families are moved all over the globe. The civilian might very well surmise that the service family is moved from one set of quarters into another set waiting especially for them at the new base.

Wrong.

Military life, with moves every three years or sooner, is not a life of easy transitions. It is true that Uncle Sam contracts with moving companies to pack and ship household goods and provides travel expenses to offset the cost of transportation for military families. However, when it comes to a roof over his head, the military man must check into the housing office at his new base and wait—sometimes up to a year or longer—for a unit designated for his rank and family size. In the meantime, he rents "on the economy," which in most locations means at a price that is more than he can afford. (Of course, if he is not required to live on base, he may prefer to rent or buy a house in the civilian community, giving him a breather from total immersion in the military life-style found on base, as well as equity in a house.)

While each base differs as to type and quality of housing available, from stately bricks to post-World War II Wherry Housing to newly

★　　　　　　★　　　　　　★

built quarters, the rules of who gets what are fairly uniform. A couple with no children is eligible for a two-bedroom unit. Add a child, add a bedroom. There tends to be a longer wait for larger units. However, if you are talking about senior officers, throw all the rules out the window. Some larger quarters are designated for base commanders—or generals—and they may be occupied only by the commander and his wife, and only for the length of time he is commander. After that they move to make room for the next commander.

If her husband dies while on active duty, the military wife must vacate quarters. Housing is only for men on active duty assigned to that particular base. Some of the more tragic stories of the Vietnam era occurred on the home front when wives of the MIA (missing in action) were evicted because they were no longer eligible for base housing. Just at the point when they could have most benefited from the closeness of the military community, they were ousted.

How well the MIA wives or the POW (prisoner of war) wives fared depended on several factors, noted one POW wife. "If you and your husband were established at a base, active in a squadron before he got shot down, the wife had networking established. The experience was hardest on the wives who had just moved to a base or had to vacate their quarters to make room for someone on active duty. It was as if your husband was erased from the roster—permanently—and no one cared. Even if the wife could get housing on a base, it meant moving the family, relocating, and starting all over without much moral support during a very trying time."

However, for those who are eligible, the military clearly takes care of its own, providing most of what a family needs: housing at a predetermined cost so there are no shocks of catastrophic rent hikes, which a civilian might face; free utilities (excluding phone), a real boon in climates requiring high heat or cooling bills; free maintenance on housing unless damage is due to the tenants' negligence; and recreational facilities that make civilians green with envy. Some fine gyms, golf courses, and Olympic-size pools are on military bases.

★　　　　　★　　　　　★

Fees charged for their use are usually much lower than at similar civilian facilities. However, it must be noted that the military consumer no longer gets a big break in prices at the base commissary or exchange. Many wives have said, in a 1989 survey in the *Air Force Times*, that they still save on staples by shopping on base but often comparison shop at neighborhood grocery or department stores for good bargains.

The major erosion of military benefits has occurred in health care. One of the major inducements for a military career was the promise of lifelong free health care for active duty and retired military members and their immediate families (under 21) at military hospitals and clinics. That is now a broken promise as the shortage of doctors forces even active duty personnel to seek civilian health care for their families. CHAMPUS, the health care insurance for the military, is mandated to pay 80 percent of incurred charges for active duty personnel and families and 75 percent for those who are retired. In the event of hospitalization, out-of-pocket costs for individuals could run into the thousands of dollars. Because of costs not covered, many military—those who can afford it—are now seeking supplemental health care insurance.

A pilot program with First Hospital Corporation (FHC) in Norfolk, Virginia, tested whether the military becomes more effective in providing support services to military families if outside agencies are utilized more fully. Alice Snyder, Ph.D., director of community education for FHC, explained that the military was finding it more difficult and expensive to provide an adequate number of military doctors, psychologists, and counselors to meet family needs. In this program, after family members seeking medical or mental health care are evaluated by base personnel, FHC helps them select a civilian care-giver within CHAMPUS guidelines. Snyder emphasized that FHC carefully monitors the client, the quality of civilian support, and the cost. According to Snyder, the savings to the military over the past three years of the program have been considerable.

★                                        ★                                        ★

In spite of the erosion of some of the benefits, it still sounds as if living in base housing is like living in paradise: all of your needs are taken care of, and there are no money worries. But as all consumers know, when something looks that good you check for hidden costs. While it is true that the military wife in many ways seems to have more than her civilian sister, she also pays a price for living on base.

On one hand she gives up a lot of freedom for security. Even if she bought every stick of furniture with her own money, she cannot authorize a military-contracted move. Either the military member must sign for all moves or he must sign a power of attorney giving her permission to act in his stead. She has to abide by the housing rules, which tend to be stricter than for civilian rentals, detailing such things as what kind of picture hooks can be used, what color she can paint the interior of "her" house, and the manner in which she must maintain the lawn. Failure to obey housing regulations can reflect on a man's service record. A civilian landlord who encounters difficulty with tenants can resort to the police or civilian courts. In the military, the landlord is Uncle Sam, who not only can evict but can bring the military member up on charges that could result, in extreme cases, in loss of rank and pay.

The quality of life for a military wife depends on her attitude. It's hard for farm girls to adjust to neighbors on either side. City girls resent the isolation of bases built in sparsely settled North Dakota. Even postings to Hawaii and Germany—just to mention two travel destinations sought after by civilians—don't please everyone. One wife said of Hawaii that she "couldn't wait to get off the rock." She said she felt safer in housing and didn't want to get out among the unfriendly locals. But another wife used her time in the Islands learning all she could about local culture. You could listen to two other wives: one praising Germany, another who hated the place and the people. It was hard to believe the women were talking about the same place. And it wasn't a matter of pay grade, either. One enlisted wife didn't have a great deal of money when she lived in Germany but she and her husband were "adopted by the family next door as if they were our grandparents. They taught me so much about their customs. We still keep in touch."

Having a chance to travel and live in company towns all over the States as well as overseas has been a source of enrichment for many military wives. But military housing did not always exist. It was a concept that evolved gradually until today the married military expect Uncle Sam to provide for them. Certainly today's quarters and living conditions are far better than those encountered on the prairies by early military wives. Yet for all the improvements, military wives are finding they still must make do with what is available. Thank goodness it is no longer tents—or they might find themselves raising their families under canvas.

## A Historical Perspective: Sod Houses and Lean-tos

Until well into the twentieth century, the military was a single man's outfit. From the time of the Revolutionary War military officers were provided quarters free of charge or else received stipends to cover housing and fuel costs. Through the nineteenth century, and well into the twentieth, housing the troops was the prime consideration of the military—not providing for the families. For any rank, the housing situation was bleak. If a woman chose to follow her husband, she made do with what she found.

The "elegance" found at the more settled forts didn't exist at the edges of the frontier. Shacks, lean-tos, tents, and hastily constructed cabins were made into homes. Beginning a life in the wilderness was never dull—it required an abundance of energy and a tremendous ability to cope with the unexpected. In 1867, Alice Blackwell Baldwin set out with her husband for Fort Harker, Kansas. She wrapped herself in robes and blankets and piled straw around her feet for protection from the bitter cold. The canvas top to the horse-drawn ambulance was pulled tight in back; it was open in front so her husband could see to drive. At the end of the first day's journey, she

\*                                    \*                                    \*

was comforted by his words, "There, my dear, behold the site of your future home; we will soon be there." She peered out to see what she had been seeing all day—thick, fast-falling snow, blanketing a bleak, flat countryside. She saw no buildings or signs of a fort until they were pointed out to her. Stovepipes jutted up through the snow; mounds marked the sites of barracks buried in the snowdrifts. She was dismayed. Her first house was nothing more than a dugout.

"When I first entered my new abode I gazed with disgusted disappointment around the bare, squalid room," Alice Baldwin wrote in her diary. "Its conveniences were limited to one camp chair, two empty candle boxes, and a huge box stove, red with rust and grime, its hearth gone and the space filled with a tobacco-stained hill of ashes, the peak of which was surmounted by 'chewed-out quids' . . . the sordid interior filled me with gloom, scarcely lessened by the four-pane glass window, dirty, dim, and curtainless."

As she explored her first home as a military wife, she found little to comfort her. The kitchen held a stove and cooking utensils laid out on the dirt floor. A packing box served as her table. She had to bend low to pass from the kitchen to her "drawing room," which had a "board floor, unplaned and full of slivers. Canvas covered the ceiling and dirt sides. It sagged slightly in the center and trembled under the scampering feet of pack rats and prairie mice. The canvas cover not quite extending on one end, the pack rats would perch on the beams, rear up on their hind legs, with their bushy tails hanging below, and survey me with their beady eyes." At one end of the "drawing room" gray army blankets were hung to partition off space for a bedroom. She cut a tiny hole in one of the blankets so that she "could peep at anyone who called whenever I sought privacy or had retired for the night."

It is quite obvious that the military made no concessions for rank. Housing was not only scarce but spartan. Living accommodations differed from fort to fort. While providing housing was not part of military regulations, housing was gradually built. At Fort Leaven-

★                                    ★                                    ★

worth in 1846, only commissioned officers were provided with housing, and a married enlisted man either had to build a cabin or purchase one from a soldier being transferred.

In spite of the apparent hardships—and dangers—of frontier life, enlisted men's wives did accompany their men and endured in a variety of abodes. At Fort Sill, Oklahoma, in 1870, married soldiers and their families lived in tents; at Fort Dodge, as late as 1875, married soldiers made their homes in dugouts or sod buildings along the riverbank. At Camp McDowell, Arizona, enlisted families found shelter in tumble-down abode huts characterized by the post surgeon as "unfit to live in." For these enlisted wives the quality of housing had improved little since Revolutionary War times.

The concept of providing a house for the duration of a man's assignment was not to occur until the twentieth century. Because houses were not allotted on a first come, first served basis but according to rank, a higher-ranking officer could commandeer more spacious quarters, forcing the family living in them to move. The term "falling bricks" was coined to describe this era of uncertainty. It was common at the turn of the century for a military wife to move in, paint rooms, work hard to make a house into a home with personal touches, and perhaps plant rose bushes—only to see those blooms enjoyed by the wife whose husband outranked hers. There is no date given as to when this practice ceased, but eventually it did. In today's military, housing assignments are for the duration of the military man's tour at each particular base.

In earlier times, many officers' families lived a life of ease, waited on by servants. Colonel R. Ernest Dupuy recalls: "The Army [officer] wife of 1904 led a more leisurely life in garrison than her sisters of today. She had a servant, of course; nearly all American middle-class families had servants in those days. And the government houses were built that way; with big kitchens, butler's pantries, and third-floor servants' quarters. She didn't have to spend hours in line to shop, although at times she might visit the commissary to choose groceries

★                              ★                              ★

and meats. But it was much simpler to write the order out in the book she left on the back porch to be picked up by the QM [quartermaster] messenger who passed daily. And before noon the groceries would be delivered."

In order to live this life of comparative luxury, an officer's family often needed an additional income to augment the military pay. For until the twentieth century, when housing allowances and moving expenses were paid by the government, all moves and housing costs were borne entirely by the family.

## THE CHANGES BEGIN

In 1907 Army and Navy officers for the first time received a stipend for heat and lighting costs added to their housing allowance. The next substantial increase of monies occurred in 1920 when the government authorized payment for officers' moves. However, as any military family will attest even today, the actual cost of moving always exceeds the amount allowed. In the last few years this reimbursement has been refined further to include a weight allowance for shipping household goods calculated according to pay grade with greater weight allowances allocated to senior officers. And the service member is paid so many cents per mile and per diem to offset transportation costs for his wife and dependent children.

After World War II ended, and the numbers of troops stabilized with many more married troops than was formerly the case, there was a growing realization that the military had to house married military and their families. Many times conditions were appalling. The first major building projects after the war were the construction of Wherry and Capehart Housing at selected bases. Mention Wherry Housing to military folks who served during that era, and most remember units that were woefully inadequate and cramped. Most of the units were flat-roofed and small with old-fashioned kitchens and bathrooms and uniformly black-tiled floors. But in the times in which they were built, they were considered desirable housing. They lasted,

**19**

and remained in use, well into the era when spaciousness was considered a necessity. As the years went by and these units continued to be used, they were usually designated "substandard," and full housing allotments were not charged for them (see Appendix). In the next decade Capehart Housing came to mean more spacious housing, usually ranch-style duplexes, with more livable floor plans and storage areas. Capehart Housing was usually reserved for families of officers and higher ranking enlisted. On bases where space was critical, four- and eight-plex housing units were built to accommodate the largest numbers of families in the least amount of space.

Today a service member can expect to find standardization of housing, but he cannot expect each base to have equal amounts of "good" housing. Some bases, located in areas of powerful political pull, have adequate numbers of units that are fairly new and beautifully maintained. One such area is Charleston, South Carolina. In the 1960s and 1970s, brand new quarters were constructed for Navy and Air Force families. If the husband was a senior enlisted or officer and if a family could survive the long wait to get in, they lived out the remainder of the tour in air-conditioned comfort. As one chief's wife said: "That housing in Charleston was one of the most comfortable I've ever lived in. Whoever designed it had common sense. The carports with screened-in porches were at opposite ends so you didn't hear other families come in. You had a little entranceway—but you didn't walk right into the living room. The kitchen window gave me a view of the street. And there were trees and curved streets. It was a good place—almost like living in the suburbs."

It is the young enlisted who encounter the most difficulty. "We lived in really horrible places," said the wife of a young sailor. "Can you imagine living in huge buildings containing families just squashed together on a little bit of land? Once you were inside it was great—a lot of room, storage, and that kind of stuff. But outside it was murder. I don't remember how often military police were called because of the fights. There was no place for the kids to play—unless it was out in

*              *              *

the street. Some women were never home and their kids ran free. Others were home but never checked on their kids. When the kids massacred each other then the adults would get into it. What a mess. I was almost scared to go out to my car at night."

## THE BLEAK PICTURE

More than one hundred years have passed since 1867 when Army wife Alice Blackwell Baldwin moved into her squalid one-room dugout. By the next century much had changed in military technology, yet little had changed in housing for the military wife. She would be housed in whatever was available. Worldwide, the military services and the Department of Defense operated approximately 390,000 sets of quarters for an estimated 1.6 million families. The problems encountered are essentially twofold: lack of quarters (an estimated 75 percent of those eligible can't get on-base housing) and quality of the quarters. A majority of the military are living in housing built in the 1950s and 1960s and the fifty-three thousand quarters built since 1970. The Air Force estimates that eighty thousand Capehart houses built in the 1950s are still in use. Budget cuts slowed housing renovations in 1988. Air Force funding was cut by 18 percent in 1988 and an average of 24 percent over the previous five years.

One of the Department of Defense's top housing officials noted that the DOD does an especially poor job for the families of junior enlisted. Fewer than 6 percent of the four hundred thousand married service members E-4 and below live in government quarters. That means 376,000 enlisted *have* to find housing elsewhere in the civilian community that may be either too expensive or substandard, such as tents outside the base at Monterey, California; dilapidated apartments over Korean bars in Wahiawa, Hawaii; tiny rooms in Japan or in stairwell tenements in Germany.

Overseas, the Department of Defense estimates that 48 percent of military families are inadequately housed. The devalued dollar and rising costs in Germany and Japan make it especially difficult for the enlisted to live overseas in any degree of comfort. In one report the DOD especially cited Korea and the Philippines as having unreliable public utilities and serious health hazards in off-base housing. The DOD minimum standards require housing to have "hot and cold running water, one flushable toilet, electrical service, a heating system if the climate requires it, and a minimum number of bedrooms to ensure that no more than two dependents share a room. A one-bedroom home must be at least 550 square feet, a two-bedroom home must be at least 750 square feet, and a three-bedroom home at least 960 square feet." With those figures as guidelines, it's easy to surmise how meager are the surroundings the majority of enlisted are forced to call home.

One marine wife sent a letter to the editor of the *Air Force Times*, with a story of what enlisted people must put up with in overseas housing. "For someone who is single or for the moneyed few, it [Okinawa] is a paradise," she wrote. "For the average marine and his family on accompanied tour, it is a different story. We spent three years there. Our house on Makiminato [a marine base] was substandard. Water ran down the walls during typhoon season. In the winter, the wind blew straight through the windows and the furnace didn't work. If you wanted air conditioners, you bought them yourself. Only a very few new housing units on Kuewae [base housing] had the greatly appreciated air-conditioning. . . . For a year, we had water only a few hours every other day because of water rationing." [Makiminato was finally closed in March 1987.]

Following a nineteen-day, four-country trip overseas in 1989, Representative Beverly B. Byron, a Democrat from Maryland and chair of the military personnel and compensation subcommittee of the House Armed Services Committee, said she was rethinking the idea that military families belong overseas with military members. She and other members of a delegation found unreasonably high rents and leases. Young servicemen and their families were suffering the most. While the cost of living in Italy, Spain, Germany, and Iceland

★                                      ★                                      ★

(where a large number of Americans are stationed) was high, the most incredible situation was found in Naples, Italy.

According to Byron, "People are living in low-quality, high-rent buildings. . . . In Naples, we are paying absolutely exorbitant rent for substandard facilities for our naval personnel stationed there, including a high school, a hospital, and an enlisted barracks sitting in an active volcano crater and an earthquake zone."

Instead of landlords working to improve the quality of life, she noted, they were ". . . lobbying Congress to prevent the Navy from relocating."

## THE MILITARY MOVES ON THE PROBLEM

Faced with the horrendous statistics of inadequate and poor housing and the numbers of the volunteer military who cite housing problems as one of the main reasons for getting out of the service, Congress authorized the release of construction money to build nine thousand new units in 1986. Even with the new units, the services estimate they are 61,000 units short of meeting on-base housing requirements for careerists, with the housing deficit growing by eleven thousand units between fiscal years 1985 and 1986.

An additional thrust to alleviate problems in housing has been to study areas of existing housing and determine how they can be made more livable. Just one such example (out of many the military has instituted to make needed changes) is Bellevue, a small community near Washington, D.C., of some four hundred Navy and Marine Corp families. The Military Family Resource Center, a national clearinghouse for military information, noted in its newsletter that Bellevue was kept in use because of the great need for housing in the Washington area. It was the only alternative for the young, lower-pay grades. According to one researcher, Bellevue had been a "community of discontent, marked by fear and unhappiness" when a study was first done on the community. As a result of the study, changes made in 1979 included establishing a United Service Organization Center in

**23**

the community and offering health clinics and other support services to the families. A small newspaper was founded to disseminate news as well as to help unify residents in this self-help project. This approach, of studying a problem area and then introducing programs and services, has been followed by the military in recent years in an attempt to improve quality of life.

Another example is of a much newer housing area built in Hawaii that experienced a multitude of problems. When completed in 1978, Aliamanu Crater Housing contained twelve thousand people in twenty-seven hundred units in a crater measuring one mile long by half a mile wide isolated from the surrounding civilian community. Crater Housing was built in increments—but without any support services in place. An earlier 1974 DOD report noted unavoidable adverse effects including ". . . the social impact of increased population density on the regional community." If a family could afford only one car, the wife's option was the local bus system, which ran infrequently, or relying on friends for transportation. The location imposed a real hardship for women needing to keep appointments at Tripler Army Medical Center just a few miles away, noted a social worker. Since there was no child care in the Crater Housing, it took an unbelievable total of eight hours for women to travel less than two miles back and forth to check a child into a base nursery at Fort Shafter, change buses to one traveling to the clinic at Tripler Army Medical Center, wait to see a doctor, then reverse the procedure to get home. By 1987, improvements included a minimart, chapel complex with meeting facilities, and recreation complex—all of which helped defuse serious problems and began the process of cementing a feeling of community.

One of the latest steps to ease the plight of the young enlisted is to bring outreach services into civilian housing. At Fort Carson, Colorado, 11,000 of the 19,000 troops are married with the majority living in widely scattered civilian communities because only 1,826 enlisted

★               ★               ★

quarters are available. Troops are deployed an average of twenty-two weeks a year on field training exercises, compounding the problem.

Al Hepford, director of the Mountain Post's Family Support Division, noted ". . . our families face a lot of stress and anxiety. And many times the family has only one car, which the soldier needs to get to work, so the family becomes more and more isolated. And the more isolated, the more stress."

To help alleviate the situation the outreach service added a van in September 1988, which goes out into the various communities with information about base services, recreation, education, medical care, and supplemental programs.

## THE BOTTOM LINE

After more than three years of interviewing and researching, it is quite obvious to the authors that Uncle Sam faces tremendous problems housing his families. There have been serious attempts to work out solutions. However, it would seem that the bottom line is self-reliance and self-preservation, for in spite of all the improvements completed and planned for—including family programs—the military family today must essentially fend for itself. Each move depletes the family's savings, for the government allowances fall far short of covering actual expenses. One survey noted that the major complaint of officers' wives is that this reimbursement never comes near compensating for all out-of-pocket expenses. There are many military families who can only afford the barest necessities, much less paying out of pocket for expensive moves. And we have not even covered the stress caused by each move that is felt most strongly by the military wife.

A team of researchers published their findings of civilian moves in a paper titled "Women's Perceived Stress and Well-Being Following Voluntary and Involuntary Relocation." The team noted that "results indicated that involuntary movers felt significantly less control and had lower levels of satisfaction with the relationship with their spouses than did voluntary movers." It was interesting that "those respondents

**25**

who moved involuntarily have significantly lower levels of perceived control over their lives than those moving voluntarily. Conceivably, this lack of control extends to decisions about moving as well as to other areas of the respondents' lives." While the military wife is consulted by the husband about choices for his next move, she actually has little to say. Uncle Sam sends them where they are needed—not necessarily where they want to go.

There needs to be more than a Band-Aid approach to improving military housing, but building more units obviously is an expensive proposition. And, it might well be asked, is that the best solution? If the military wants to keep retention figures high in the all-volunteer force, changes have to be made. Suggestions made by experts hired by the government to research the problem include: working with more experimental programs, such as leasing housing units from the private sector; moving families less often and stabilizing them with home porting in which the troops are moved less frequently; not moving a family unless it can be guaranteed appropriate quarters at the new base; less homogeneity within the housing areas so that younger families will have older, hopefully more mature families as peers. One of the more drastic suggestions is to return to the mandate of a single man's military below the E-4 level. Not doing so reinforces the vicious cycle of poverty. Another suggestion is to allow wives to have more of a say in how their housing is structured and maintained, as is being done through the self-rule concept of the mayoral program in place on Army bases. This program elects a mayor from among housing residents to listen to problems on a grass-roots level and pass suggestions to the base commander for solutions.

There are no easy answers. However, many of these suggestions need not cost additional monies. Home porting, for example, means less moves, less cost. Not moving as often provides a more stable family life. Studying a problem, then involving residents in the solution, results in the formation of a more cohesive community and

★                                    ★                                    ★

less of a welfare-state approach. The authors applaud these attempts in the last few years as an honest effort to improve living conditions and the quality of life for military families. But much more needs to be done before Uncle Sam's brides can call housing home.

★ ★ ★

"When I die, I hope to come back as a member of the Officers' Wives' Club and do nothing but loll about the pool all day. That's heaven."

—OFFICER'S SAYING

Within each company town the military gathers at its clubs for traditional rites of "happy hours," "hail and farewells," promotion parties, "dining in," and formal dress balls. Even after "duty" hours, the glut of men in uniform gives the impression that work hours never end but simply ooze from office to club. Aside from a preponderance of uniforms, these military clubs are similar to civilian clubs or private fraternal organizations in which membership is restricted, dues are often required, and wives can only be adjunct members. However, while it is usually unimportant whether a civilian joins a club or not, for the military officer, joining the officers' club is a must for promotion.

There are many organizations on a military base—squadrons, ship or flight crews, chapel affiliates, scouts and sports groups—but there are only two social classes, officer and enlisted. Within these two distinct social classes are three clubs: the officers' club, the noncommissioned officers' (NCO) club (in the Navy noncommissioned officers are CPOs or chief petty officers, the top grades of the enlisted ranks), and the enlisted men (EM) club, for the lower four ranks of enlisted. (See Appendix for explanation of ranks.) In addition, the Navy has the CPO clubs which was the exclusive domain of the chief petty officers (E-7, E-8 and E-9.) There was even separate chief's housing. Now other services have gone to the Top Three Graders Club which is the equivilent of the CPO club.

Enter the wives. Picture them sequined and elegant at formal dress balls and power dressed for various functions of the wives' clubs. These clubs exist on the basis of exclusivity, accepting each woman

★                 ★                 ★

for, or barring her from, membership not on her own merits or education but simply on the basis of her husband's rank or lack of it. Again, there are three clubs: one for officers' wives (OWC), one for NCO wives (NCOWC), and one for enlisted wives (EWC).

While wives of all ranks mingle at chapel functions, on Little League or soccer fields, and at the rare traditional event that brings officer and enlisted together, the women remain segregated in the military's two distinct social worlds. As one colonel's wife remarked, "Even if an extremely bright, gifted, college-educated woman from the civilian upper classes should elect to marry an enlisted, that's her mistake. Unless her husband promotes to officer rank, she is condemned to a life in the military outside of the officer's superior social hierarchy."

The term "military wives' clubs" applies only to those formal women's organizations having a constitution, by-laws, elected officers, and advisory board, regularly scheduled meetings, and dues. All branches of the United States military permit the chartering of military wives' clubs. These clubs, found only on military installations and not affiliated with any civilian women's clubs, may be the only organizations supposedly *for* women that are absolutely controlled by men. A military wife may not start a club on her own but needs permission from the base commanding officer (rarely a female). In addition, a husband must give his permission and sponsor his wife's membership. On some bases a wife's club membership card is not issued in her own name but in her husband's name and contains the initials DW—Dependent Wife. At Langely Air Force Base, Virginia, for example, information for wives' club members is mailed to the sponsor, addressed with the husband's name and rank, not the wife's name. Should he divorce her, her membership terminates.

Additionally, each club is closely chaperoned. A senior officer's wife (many times the base commander's wife) is required to serve as an "adviser" to ensure that club activities are restricted to doing good for the military. So there will never be a military wives' club cam-

★                              ★                              ★

paigning for gay rights, picketing the military for better pay, or working to obtain medical benefits for divorced military wives. (The one exception is the National Military Family Association covered at the end of the chapter.) Instead, a great deal of the wives' time will be spent in acceptable "keep 'em busy and out of our hair" activities such as bridge, cultural outings, decorating the club for monthly luncheons and dinners, fashion shows, and a host of other time-consuming, mind-numbing activities.

Opinions regarding the merit of military wives' clubs tend to be quite strong. Women who do not support them say the clubs do little to promote interest in areas outside of those connected with the traditional female stereotypes: table decorations, flower arranging, recipes, and fashion shows. These wives resent the pressure (both subtle and overt) brought to bear on them to join and participate. Wives who support the club concept say they are extremely valuable for companionship and volunteer effort.

In fact, one of the major functions of any wives' club (some say the only redeeming function) is providing volunteers for a variety of charitable activities, a tradition begun by Martha Washington and her ladies and formalized in 1780 by Esther De Berdt Reed, wife of Washington's adjutant general, into an association of women from Pennsylvania, Maryland, New Jersey, and Delaware. Since then, wives' club members have promoted the idea of women as volunteers and seem to find the idea that some women would prefer to be paid for their labor discomforting and almost immoral. Most clubs sponsor, as well as manage, base thrift shops. On some posts, wives' club members also sponsor gift shops, provide nursery services, help staff family service centers, volunteer time for the Red Cross and USO, organize craft fairs and Christmas gift-wrapping services. Money earned from thrift/gift shops and other fund-raising activities (thousands of dollars each year) is used in support of both base and community projects, including orphanages, specialized schools, clin-

★ ★ ★

ics, playground equipment, library needs, youth activities, and scholarships.

Another major purpose of the wives' clubs is to welcome newcomers and make them feel a part of the military community. This, however, is where many wives feel let down. Most wives' clubs do not function as an equivalent of the civilian Welcome Wagon. Seldom does anyone from the wives' club welcoming committee personally call on a newcomer. Usually a mimeographed "welcome packet" of information about the base is sent to her. Usually, if a wife wishes to actively participate, she must go to a luncheon or a "hail and farewell" coffee on her own initiative. Not always is she welcomed with open arms. Cliques have formed and she, after all, is an outsider, a newcomer. At one overseas base, women were cautioned, "Don't go to a luncheon unless you know you have someone to sit with. Otherwise you could be left standing against the wall by yourself." The new wife is neither sought after nor recruited but must make her own niche.

For the wife who takes the bull by the horns and becomes an active and contributing member of a wives' club, there will be an endless round of cultural, recreational, and social activities. In addition, the wife will hostess in her home an infinite number of "required" dinners and parties. While these social functions may seem no more than a treadmill of trivial activities to civilians, for many military wives—especially officers' wives—they are vital to the wives' own well-being in this closed community and, perhaps more important, to their husbands' careers. A large number of officers' wives indicated that their husbands seldom asked if they wanted to attend club functions or have guests in their homes. The wives were merely given dates for events. The message was clear: you will do this.

How few are the women of this generation who can fully understand the power wielded by the wives of the "Old Guard." When a colonel or Navy captain's wife announced she was having a tea and assigned a dish for each junior wife to bring, there were no excuses short of hospitalization. Each wife did as she was told. Obviously,

*  *  *

many men and women of this Old Guard will take a dim view of anyone who challenges military tradition as today's military wife is doing.

"Are you the women who stirred up all the trouble for the Air Force about being allowed to work?" asked a retired Army colonel's wife of the authors. She added that she and her husband had agreed that she couldn't give a interview for any publication that "might say anything negative about the Army." However, many other men and women are aware that the military, like American society, has changed greatly over the past forty years and realize that the military spouse is attempting to keep pace with these changes. So today's officer's wife is not in as rigid a society as was the previous generation.

On the other hand, unless she wishes to do so, Mrs. Enlisted Wife has no pressure to perform military-related social duties for her husband. For the enlisted man, climbing the social ladder is not considered important in attaining higher rank, as his promotions are primarily based on testing and job performance. Nor would many officers even consider the enlisted as having a social ladder with two hundred years of tradition viewing him as a laborer and his wife as a laundress from Soap Suds Row. Most officers and their wives are as aloof to enlisted society as royalty might be to their servants. Within this setting any further discussion of the wives' club as an important part of the military social arena will pertain only to the officer class.

Being part of this "upper crust" brings on problems. Even for the officer's wife who thoroughly enjoys club activities, there is underlying tension, a constant reminder that she is on stage. She must run a better bazaar and bring in more money than did the last chairwoman. She must watch her tongue. Everything she says or does is noted and discussed. If she says something "out of turn" or derisive, or disagrees with advice given by a "senior wife," her husband's career may be jeopardized.

One Navy wife interviewed fell apart under the pressure of just such club politics. She is now divorced after a long separation. To

**33**

regain her emotional stability and her sense of self-worth she gave up what many women would consider a lot: a beautifully furnished house filled with antiques and collectibles on commanders' row.

What caused her life to unravel? With hindsight the thirty-eight-year-old woman realized it was a combination of things: the move to a new base, her husband's long hours and increased responsibilities, and the need to "socialize with wives who didn't give a damn. I couldn't make friends, yet I had left long-time friends who cared. I never knew what to say. Or if I said something I'd get a 'That's nice, dear.' At wives' club functions I'd get nervous and then start drinking a little." Her words seemed at odds with her appearance. Carole was sharply dressed, a good-looking woman who appeared poised. "The tension at home became terrible," she remembered. "He started criticizing me, because he was being criticized by his peers for my behavior. His lectures and yelling became constant. I couldn't just stop attending functions because I was expected to be there. So when I went out, I tried to fade into the wallpaper. I'd dread going out. I couldn't stop my crying jags. It got so bad I moved out before I fell completely apart."

Of course, nothing will appear in official records about her "failure"—or his—to control her attitude. But unofficially he began hearing about her outlandish behavior. He now has a new wife, one who is performing social functions as expected.

For the officer, his wife's participation in the military social arena is critical and it may make his climb up the ladder easier. As Maureen Mylander, author of *The Generals*, states, "The social arena is the Army wife's natural habitat. If the officer aspires to higher ranks, the emphasis intensifies to 'play the game.' " This is a game played by two for it is expected that the wife be a full participant—if he is to be upwardly mobile. The military wife is seen as an adjunct of her husband; how she performs (and conforms) directly reflects on him.

One question consistently asked is, "Do all wives have to belong to the wives' club?" The *official* answer is no. When a woman marries a

★                    ★                    ★

military man, she signs no form committing her to a lifetime of service and membership.

Does wives' club membership and involvement in at home entertaining help an officer get promoted? "No!" would be the emphatic answer from the military, and this is true considering that no official requirement is made that his wife join the wives' club; no record is kept in the husband's promotion folder of his wife's attendance at wives' club functions; no one specifically says that she must continually have cocktail parties or dinners for her husband's boss, the visiting lieutenant colonel or general.

However, the more truthful answer to both questions is yes. To a large extent, what military manners author Nancy Shea said twenty years ago applies today. "There is no law making it obligatory for an officer to join the officers' club but he is expected to support the activities of his unit. The same holds true for an officer's wife; it is her duty to join and pay her dues. . . . Understand there is no regulation compelling a wife to join . . . but she is expected to do so."

It would seem that it is the rare wife who can totally ignore the wives' club, for wives perceive pressure and feel any social inadequacy on their part will reflect negatively on their husbands' careers. Of course, there are no statistics kept, no list of men who have resigned commissions, failed to be promoted or, conversely, have soared to top grades without their wives' sociability quotient coming into play. Maureen Mylander feels that while a wife "cannot cause her husband's advance . . . she can prevent it." The military promotes those who conform. And there is definite pressure to conform.

Nancy, a slim aerobics instructor and an Army officer's bride of only ten months, felt she had to join the wives' club to help her husband. "I come from an Air Force family, and my mother was always active in the club. In fact, I feel that my dad was promoted to full colonel because of my mother's activities. If she hadn't been such a good hostess and so active, he might not have made it." She paused to carefully choose the right words. "I don't mean that he wasn't well qualified or that he didn't deserve the promotion. However, I think people saw how capably she arranged functions and dinners, and because she was so capable, everyone assumed he was equally as capable in his job."

An authors' survey of officers' wives supports Nancy's explanation. Very few of the wives mentioned personal satisfaction as a reason for joining wives' clubs. Sixty-three percent of the wives had become members of the OWC either because their husbands had encouraged them to do so or because they felt it was required in order to help their husbands be promoted.

Explaining why she had joined the OWC in the late fifties, Theresa, wife of a lieutenant general, summed up what many other wives of her era have said: "I felt there was pressure to join. It was simply the thing you did."

This, of course, was not overt pressure. She was experiencing the peer pressure felt strongest when other wives said, "Of course, you are coming to the OWC luncheon next Tuesday," or when she received a call indicating that she had been "volunteered" to serve on a committee to plan the craft fair. The implication was clear—naturally a wife would join and participate. The question remains: would Theresa's husband have made general if she had not proved her worth?

Entertaining at home can be equally important for the man moving into senior rank and hoping to go all the way to the top. The negative side of entertaining is reflected in the comments of a lieutenant colonel's wife. "I'm always having people to dinner who I don't know and don't want to know," she complained. "And it puts a big hole in our budget. I'll bet if we had to do this in a civilian job, he'd have an expense account. But I try not to say much to Steve because he always tells me it's necessary and that it will make his job easier. I sure hope it helps when he meets the promotion board next year. I'd hate to be the cause of him being passed over."

Having no house, household goods, or furniture seems not to be an

★　　　　　　　　★　　　　　　　　★

acceptable excuse for not entertaining. "Our household goods had already been shipped and, other than breakfast food or an occasional sandwich, we were eating every meal out," explained a lieutenant colonel's wife just back from the overseas tour on which this incident occurred. "A major was sent on temporary additional duty [TDY] for an inspection. Every evening he was at the site and we ate with him in the dining hall. He knew we were leaving in just four days, had no furniture, dishes, etc. Still, when he got back to Offutt Air Force Base (Nebraska), he complained that he had not been entertained adequately. My husband's boss, a colonel, called and really chewed him out for not properly wining and dining this guy. That really put a sour end to what had been an otherwise wonderful tour. And, of course, we are both terribly edgy about this incident maybe affecting his chances for promotion this year, maybe causing him to be passed over."

## PASSED OVER

Civilians cannot fully comprehend the shock nonpromotion holds for an officer. One of the worst things that can happen is being "passed over" for promotion to a higher rank. The officer's career is over—and the entire military system knows it. Both the man and his wife are stunned. What happened? What could have been done to prevent this castastrophe?

Counselors, military psychologists, and chaplains speak of being passed over as similar to a death of a loved one. The entire family of the officer goes through a period of mourning. The wife experiences tremendous guilt over what she perceives as her part in his failure. She spends the rest of his shortened career never quite in the center of the social climbers. Not only are current earnings and potential retirement earnings affected (figures that can total as high as several hundred thousand dollars), but the military member has basically been told he is somehow unfit. His status and the status of his wife and family have dropped considerably. There is so much stigma

**37**

attached to being passed over that those achieving promotion have difficulty relating to the unfortunate individual. Friends become former friends; co-workers pretend nothing has happened; invitations sharply decrease in number.

What happens to the military wife who worked hard to do all the right things for all of her life and yet her husband failed to be promoted? When their husbands were passed over, many of the officers' wives interviewed were debilitated by depression and guilt. It was as if they were responsible for the failure of their husbands.

"You never know if what you do as the wife really affects your husband's career," stated Mary, the wife of a passed-over lieutenant colonel. "I guess I'd have to say that while you can't break your husband's career, you can probably bend it a little if you are not the typical wife." When asked if she felt she had done something that kept her husband from being promoted to full colonel, she replied, "I really couldn't put my finger on it if I did. I thought I had at least done a minimum of clubbing and entertaining, but I always seemed to be on the outside of the cliques. I just seemed to always smile at the wrong time or not quite be in on the jokes and the latest gossip. It's probably just my imagination," she added with a shrug, "or maybe I'm—what do they call it—rationalizing. Maybe it's just sour grapes."

Another wife whose husband was not promoted to lieutenant colonel (meaning he would be forced to leave the service after twenty years, at age forty-two) stated that they were ". . . never able to quite get in with the 'movers' [the service academy grads, the elite fighters, those couples who it is generally believed will reach the top]. We just didn't fit in, and these were the men my husband worked with [who] would help each other move up the ladder. I really tried to get in with that particular clique but I always seemed to be on the fringes."

Rightly or wrongly, these women have assumed a personal responsibility for their husbands' lack of upward mobility. Regardless of whether there is any validity behind their feelings, they see their

\*                                    \*                                    \*

social acceptability (or lack of it) as having a direct bearing on their husbands' careers. There are no official guidelines, but when one has filled all of the required blocks and doesn't get promoted, the question of why may be unofficially attributed to the nebulous term "social ineptness." Military couples become indoctrinated to the idea that if you play the game correctly, the chances for promotion are improved. And a large part of the game centers around social gatherings.

## CLIQUES AND COMMANDERS' WIVES

For some wives, the club provides a moment of glory, a chance to head the base organization, either through elections or through a husband's position. Though Nancy Shea states: "[The OWC] is not a meeting place to exchange the latest gossip and rumors, or to form social cliques . . . ," in some clubs newcomers are disgruntled to find a gossip-ridden club with a clique fighting to retain its power. Like any formal organization, the club is directed by its hierarchy of officers and executive board members. The women in this hierarchy, like all individuals in leadership positions, have a certain amount of prestige and power. For many women a position in this hierarchy may be one of the major rewards of OWC participation. They tend to guard this power position jealously, especially when suggestions or ideas from newcomers threaten the status quo.

Wives living off base are also aware of the power of cliques in the clubs. "There is a distinct line between those who live on base and share the close living and those of us who live off base," said Dorothy, wife of an Air Force captain. "We know the OWC wants us to join and pay our dues; this fattens the membership roster and adds to the club's funds. When you live off base, you tend not to know any of the other women well. Every time you go to a meeting or coffee, you feel like an interloper."

To some extent Dorothy's comments were supported in the book, *Families in the Military System*, which indicated that the military wife living on post "is less likely to identify with the neighboring commu-

★                              ★                              ★

nity." The officer's wife living on base "is expected to participate more in . . . volunteer services" than is the wife who lives in the civilian community. Therefore, she establishes close ties with other on-base wives; the off-base wife remains a stranger.

In all fairness, however, it must be pointed out that in some clubs, without a dependable clique, the club would simply cease to function. One colonel's wife who was very active in the OWC explained, "With our attendance as low as it is sometimes, if we didn't have a clique of a few wives we can count on, there wouldn't be anyone at club meetings or luncheons. It's the ones who only come infrequently and don't really get to know the rest of us who point fingers and yell 'clique.' "

Next to the clique, the commanding officer's wife (COW) takes the most hits from OWC members. Her position of power as club adviser or member of the executive board comes directly from her husband's selection as a commander. Whether she relishes this position or not, she has little choice in the matter, as her duties are outlined in a "Commander's Spouse Handbook" that lists protocol and the role of the spouse in mission accomplishment. How her power within the club is handled depends on the individual woman. Some merely play their designated role as it is intended and graciously offer advice; for others, their advice is couched in direct orders: "What I want the club to do . . ." This latter type usually does not solicit or react favorably to suggestions from club members at large or other board members.

To show how far this power can go, one young lieutenant's wife, with a master's degree in counseling, had a suggestion to improve the base nursery run by an officers' wives club. However, for speaking out, she was thoroughly castigated by a Navy captain's wife on the nursery board, and her children were barred from the nursery. "My experience was a real demonstration to me of the way I am seen as an appendage of my husband and the way my performance affects him," said Deanna, the lieutenant's wife. "You have to understand that finding child care was a real nightmare. But I never thought I would

*       *       *

be asked to remove my children for objecting to graphic violence demonstrated to three-year olds. I walked in on a teacher using a flannel board to [illustrate] the part of the Hansel and Gretel story where hot oil was being poured over someone's head. I was shocked. I thought it and the cartoons were too violent for these little kids.

"In a real low-key way, I asked the chairwoman to look into it. Well, I found out later, they perceived me as a real troublemaker. 'Who is this little lieutenant's wife who has the audacity to question us?' I was told to take my children elsewhere. I even talked to the legal people to see if I had rights. I had none, they said. They could exclude people on any basis—except race. My husband's boss even called him in and told him to tell me to drop it. I never saw child care as an extension of the military," said Deanna. "I thought we were all women talking. How naive!"

Deanna learned that "senior" wives can control the wives' club, as did Georgia, the charming gray-haired wife of a retired Air Force colonel. Shortly after Georgia had been elected president of the base wives' club she was summoned by the base commander's wife. "She was a rather commanding figure herself," Georgia began, referring to the general's wife, "with a crusty way of speaking. I had only been the president a few weeks and really wasn't too sure what I had gotten myself into. Also, I was a fairly young captain's wife and wasn't used to talking with generals' wives. We were having a very pleasant conversation regarding volunteers for some wives' club activity coming up, and I mentioned that there were a couple of women who weren't too interested in helping out. Immediately the general's wife said: 'We can always get their husbands moved to another post.' This was during the Vietnam War, and I really felt bad that I had said anything. However, since the general was assigned to another base just a few weeks later, I don't think any of the men were moved."

Another wife had her whole summer ruined because she felt she couldn't say no to the wife of her husband's commander. Barbara recalls a tumultuous time in Missouri when her husband was a very

★                    ★                    ★

junior officer and she received a telephone call from the base commander's wife. "All good officers' wives should learn to play mah-jongg, dear," Barbara coos, imitating a syrupy sweet southern accent. "I had been commuting a hundred and thirty miles a day on two-lane roads to try and keep a college teaching career intact. I was so looking forward to the summer vacation period, just to sit on my backside and do nothing. Certainly I wasn't interested in concerning myself about east winds and west winds and flowers or whatever junk was involved in learning the game. Nevertheless, for weeks I dutifully went to the commander's home and learned mah-jongg with three other junior officers' wives. Each evening after a totally wasted afternoon, I went home and made my husband's life miserable by bitching like hell. I wanted to tell the commander's wife to take a flying leap, as we would have said tactfully in those long-ago days, but I knew if I did it could hurt my husband's career and, ultimately, our economic security."

## LOVE THAT CLUB

At this point, one might ask, other than the husband's career, are there any good reasons for joining the club? The answer is yes, and the mosaic of the wives' club is not complete without mentioning the women who really enjoy their club. For them the club means companionship, status, a chance to volunteer for worthwhile causes, and a sense that they are contributing to the welfare of their husbands. As they move to a new base, the club should give them easy entry into their new surroundings, a way to meet women with whom to play bridge or golf or to share similar experiences. In the club a wife knows her place and knows what is expected of her. She can find a little of the old, the familiar in her new and strange environment.

For those women who derive a sense of self-worth and sincere pleasure from helping others, volunteer opportunities are unlimited. Through volunteering the wife not only contributes to the base and the community, but she also gains self-confidence and skills that may at a future time make her employable.

★                              ★                              ★

Additionally, the mystique of the wives' club as the route to high society is so strong that even in the 1980s brand-new brides of officers just coming on post show up for that first welcoming coffee with a question, "Where can I get my calling cards?" That simple query about a social nicety that went out of vogue twenty years ago illustrates the mind-set that she has married into the upper officer class and is preparing to learn what is required of her.

In fact, the OWC members do educate young wives in the required social graces. As in any group, the older members become role models, teaching military traditions to the junior officers' wives, who take their place in the establishment. Even Jean, a savvy graduate of the University of California at Berkeley and an Army colonel's wife, recognized the savoir faire she acquired. Describing her first days as an officer's wife, she said, "I was from a small California town. I felt overwhelmed with all that was expected of me as an officer's wife. For me, the club was a training ground where others, more experienced than me, showed me how to dress and how to behave as my husband prepared for his career overseas."

Also, the OWC recaptures a little of the grandeur of past tradition with an occasional fancy dress ball or dinner tables aglitter in crystal and silver. A Marine colonel's wife, reed thin, smartly coiffed, and dressed in a pale pink silk suit, summarized in a southern accent what several wives of senior officers felt. "For us, playing the part of clubwoman is fun. Our kids are mostly gone; we're no longer short of money. I like to dress up in the middle of the day and spend several hours over a long lunch if I want to. It took us twenty-seven years in the military, but I feel like I've finally reached my station in life. I want a little of the icing on the cake and, for me, that's being able to while away my time with friends who have the same life-style and think like me, in OWC activities."

For the wives who enjoy club activity, the club provides a place to make friends, to network about base services and activities, to give wives access to the political and social part of military life. Janice,

**43**

wife of an Air Force pilot and mother of four children, is very supportive of the wives' club. "I'm quite active and try to attend regularly. I joined because I felt it would be support for me, and it would get me with adults and away from the children at least twice a month. Also, I thought this would be a good way to learn about being an officer's wife."

## THE CHANGES BEGIN

As recently as ten years ago, the thought of joining or not joining a club would not even have been considered by most officers' wives. Women married to officers not only joined "their" club but participated, some to the extent that their lives were totally immersed in the wives' club. Wives in the 1960s and 1970s were not generally employed outside the home, so it was a time of hats, white gloves, and fashion shows. The officers' wives were in step with their civilian sisters who graced the pages of hometown society pages with their teas, balls, and social functions.

Today, the double whammy of feminism and the uneasy economy have effected catastrophic changes in wives' club participation. In today's volunteer military the young officer's wife, with perhaps a better education than the older wives or career aspirations of her own, is rattling this two-hundred-year-old social cage by refusing to devote her life wholeheartedly to interminable social events. A letter to the editor of a military newspaper emphasizes this "new-found educational and career independence" of military wives and urges the Air Force wives' club to address issues of critical importance to American society rather than continue activities and publications that "consistently comprise that which is benign, social, or just plain trivial."

The officer's wife may still feel she has to join the club, but she is objecting to enforced volunteerism whereby she is told to participate, and is limiting her attendance at social events. As one wife in Hawaii lamented, "At the first meeting in the fall, forty are present, at the next meeting this attendance has dropped to twenty-five, by Thanks-

★               ★               ★

giving, you are lucky if you can regularly count on fifteen ladies."
Nor are wives as interested in being candidates for OWC offices.
While thanking those women who had agreed to run for and had been
elected to office, a four-star general's wife on an eastern base mentioned that in the Washington, D.C., area and at a large midwestern
base, no candidates had come forward. In order to attract women,
meetings have been moved from day to evening. Wives are working—
not just to keep busy but to bring in a paycheck, and they are going
to school. This new breed of officers' wife is simply saying "no" to
more than minimum participation, consequences be damned. At an
overseas base, in order to get candidates to run for OWC president,
when not one woman had stepped forward, it was proposed that the
"winner" be given free child care, a reserved parking space at the
officers' club, and a maid on days that the woman was fulfilling OWC
duties. When this "paid" position was proposed, many women decided to run. Before this idea could come to fruition, however, the
women were reminded that the OWC president should be a volunteer,
not paid.

"When my husband was commanding officer of a base in Virginia
in the seventies, my entire life revolved around social functions,"
explained Cindy, the gregarious wife of an Air Force colonel. "I
would actually come back home with only enough time to check on
the children, change clothes from a wives' club meeting, and go out
the door to another function. I never stopped to ask myself why—I
just did what was expected of me. Now I am selling real estate and
frankly don't have the time or the interest. However, I keep up my
membership and attend a few things—only because it is good for my
business to keep my contacts fresh. Otherwise, I don't think I would
bother."

These wives' comments are supported by an issue of *Off Duty*, a
magazine for military wives, in which one wife indicated that many
wives are no longer getting excited about luncheons or "putting
together a craft item for a bazaar. . . . Participation in wives' clubs

**45**

★              ★              ★

everywhere is declining." The author stated wives' clubs might encourage better participation and meet the needs of the wives by asking what types of programs are really wanted. She also suggested that club meetings need to accommodate schedules of working women and back-to-schoolers.

Is employment, then, an acceptable excuse for nonparticipation in OWC activities? Author Maureen Mylander feels that if a wife is employed and does not participate in base and community activities to any great extent, ". . . the effects on her husband's fortunes [will depend] upon why she works." Apparently the military will condone a wife working ". . . if her husband is overseas, if they need the money for their children's college education, or if the family lives in a costly area such as Washington, D.C." However, choosing to work because she thinks the usual activities open to wives are demeaning or represent so much "make-work" is not acceptable.

Some wives do feel the wives' club activities are make-work and are simply no longer interested in what many wives' clubs have to offer. An Army wife stated: "I work and am also taking classes working toward my degree, but that's not the whole story. I just don't feel that I can waste my time deciding which type of decorations to use for the April luncheon or going to crystal bingo [in which prizes of crystal are awarded]. The wives' clubs are still so traditional, still doing what their counterparts were doing fifty years ago. Oh, I always have my husband put my name on the wives' club membership lists when he joins the officers' club, but I haven't gone to a meeting in ten years. Usually someone calls me when it's cookie baking time, and I always try to bake my quota of cookies for the bake sale or the Christmas cookie exchange. Once I was 'volunteered' for some project and told if I couldn't make it to delegate the job to someone else. Delegate! That's another word for coerce. I did the project because I didn't want to force another woman like I had been forced. But I didn't want people to say I wasn't supporting my husband. I also will do some volunteer work, if there's a good cause involved, although I'm

&#42;          &#42;          &#42;

the type that feels women should be paid for their labor. I won't do volunteer work to pay for name tags or game prizes; if the club is raising money for scholarships or some fund that aids everyone on the base, then I'll give my time. But I really do think the days of the OWC are numbered."

One young Air Force captain's wife was not as tactful. Sitting behind a large desk sign that proclaimed her the administrative assistant to the director of a large university program, she said to one of the authors: "When all of you old women are gone, the OWC as it is today will cease to exist. Many of us today are involved in good jobs and can't take the time to attend inane coffees." Questioned about the effect her attitude would have on her husband's military career, she replied, "Sooner or later the military is going to have to evaluate men on *their* merits, not their wives." Her comments indicate the current trend of thinking among some of the younger wives.

Another change facing the wives' clubs is that on many bases Family Services has usurped some of the club's duties by providing information to newcomers, volunteers for base activities, and information for wives regarding available base services. If this trend continues, wives' club activities will soon be relegated solely to the social arena.

However, while the days of the wives' clubs seem to be numbered at military bases in the United States, participation in overseas clubs is still good. Apparently isolation from the extended family, scarcity of employment for military spouses, and culture shock sends military wives scurrying to the OWC, hoping to find comfort and companionship from their peers. Also, for wives of retired officers, the OWC helps them retain old ties or, for those who have moved near unfamiliar bases, establish new contacts. Today at many OWC functions the older officer's wife is much in evidence, a phenomenon that might be characterized as "the graying of the OWC."

In the final analysis, it is almost impossible to reach a conclusion about the impact of military wives' clubs. Women surveyed and

**47**

interviewed seemed to either love them or hate them. It would appear that for the enlisted wife, there is little pressure for her to join because of her husband; her rewards apparently come from community service and companionship. For the officer's wife, traditional feeling largely prevails that she must join, for her benefit and for her husband's. Regardless of whether military wives' clubs are considered beneficial and vital or archaic, clique-ridden, and trivial, they continue to be a functioning part of the military life-style. Although many members no longer actively support these organizations, it is interesting to note that for various reasons their names remain on club rosters. As a "camp follower"—highly mobile, often lonely, sometimes bored—the military spouse tends to find companionship mostly among others of her kind. Whether she joins the wives' club to gain immediate pleasure from activities with other wives or for the purpose of furthering both her and her husband's careers, the purpose of the club is fulfilled.

## THE NEW CLUBS—THE LOBBYISTS

In addition to the wives' clubs, which remain primarily social organizations, two powerful wives' groups have sprung up to correct perceived wrongs. One is the National League of Families of American Prisoners and Missing in Southeast Asia and the other is the National Military Family Association. Both groups cut across the officer/ enlisted distinction and have as their members wives and families from all ranks and all services. These organizations have had a powerful impact on changing military policy over the past twenty years.

The League of Families was incorporated in the District of Columbia on May 28, 1970. It originated on the West Coast in the late 1960s through the efforts of the wife of the ranking prisoner of war who felt that the government's policy of keeping a low profile on the POW/ MIA issue was unjustified. At the time the government pressured families not to go public with their stories. The first POW/MIA story was published in October 1968. As a result of the publicity, families

★                              ★                              ★

began communicating with each other. As wives networked among themselves—and their first efforts were word of mouth without help from the military—a cohesive group began to form that eventually evolved into the league.

In 1989, the league had a membership of 3,600 with coordinators in most of the fifty states for its ongoing efforts. As of May 26, 1989, 2,357 Americans remained missing or unaccounted for in Southeast Asia. The league says: "The U.S. government places its highest priority on the live prisoner issue, which is at the forefront of negotiations and the intelligence effort." In his inaugural message, President George Bush addressed the plight of Americans "who are held against their will in foreign lands and Americans who are unaccounted for." In a later clarification he told the press of his "absolute determination not to forget" the POWs or MIAs.

One POW wife remembered those oppressive times when the military clamped down on releasing any information, even to wives and family members. For almost two years she heard nothing about the status of her husband. Finally, she heard that he was a prisoner in Southeast Asia. "The league was the first group of military wives who banded together to oppose this military policy. You have to remember the climate of the times. It was an unpopular war. It was as if we were outcasts. We had to fight for everything we got, even though we were military wives and had a good background of service to our country. Once we asked our OWC for assistance in our letter-writing campaign. Our request was questioned by the base commander. He even questioned us about setting up a table outside the commissary to collect petitions. I have some feeling of bitterness that we could not get more from our government and that people were so reluctant to help us."

The National Military Family Association began in 1969 when a group of military wives and widows organized to advocate financial security for survivors of military personnel and retirees. Throughout the 1970s, NMFA testified before Congress on the Survivor Benefit

**49**

Plan, Dependency and Indemnity Compensation, and the retention of commissary privileges. NMFA has conducted and published two important surveys. The first was a survey of more than three thousand military family members in Europe published as "Final Report: Military Spouse and Family Issues." The Department of Defense implemented most of the report's recommendations, including a funded travel allowance for dependent college students whose parents are stationed overseas and a Military Family Policy Office established in 1987. The second, "Hawaii Final Report," was a quality of life survey conducted by NMFA's Hawaii chapter and published in 1987.

NMFA's main thrust is education of military families about their rights and benefits and the policymakers about the unique aspects of military life. During the 100th Congress NMFA was active in developing and implementing policies that affect military families. Among the many actions NMFA took were: influencing Congress to reject "users' fees" for military medical clinics; persuading Congress to vote down a bill discriminating against the hiring of military spouses as DoDDS (Department of Defense Dependent Schools) teachers; requesting DOD affirmation that spouses may choose gainful employment, continuing education, volunteer work, or other activities without command pressure (DOD issued directives in 1987 and 1988), and encouraging development of in-home child care on military installations (all services were issued regulations, and in-home programs began by late 1988).

After more than two hundred years of traditional club society, today's wives are doing more than dawdling by the pool. Through their lobbying they are having an impact not only on Congress but also on the military.

&#9733;    &#9733;    &#9733;

"I have felt almost too wretched to write letters for the last ten days. Indeed, I have never been so unhappy in my life . . . This uncertainty of everything . . . this not knowing or hearing anything is the hardest thing to bear. . . . I am very anxious and worried about my dear husband. . . ."

—Emily Fitzgerald McCorkle
Letter Home to Her Mother
August 30, 1877
Fort Lapwai, Idaho

★          ★          ★

The women swirled past another military wife name Emily as if she were invisible. The year was 1977. All the other women in the barnlike commissary seemed to have a sense of purpose, a destination, important things to do. No one gave her a nod, a smile, or a hello. As a newcomer in town, she saw no familiar faces.

Emily was totally alone, killing time.

Time was the enemy for this pretty nineteen-year-old: she had to survive six months alone in the bustling Navy town of Norfolk. Her husband had just enough time to move her into an apartment complex and start an allotment that would send her most of his pay as an E-3 while he was deployed on a ship steaming toward the Persian Gulf (see Appendix, Pay Schedule). Once he left, she was on her own. She knew no one. No one in this town of strangers knew her. The neighbors in the run-down housing area seemed preoccupied with young children. There was no system like the civilian Welcome Wagon that would personally visit this very junior enlisted wife. A senior enlisted man and his family might be greeted on arrival, most certainly a senior officer and his family would be met. But not the young enlisted. She was on her own.

"They said we were supposed to have a sponsor greet us when we first arrived in Norfolk. But no one did," Emily said with a tentative smile. When she smiled, her whole face lit up and she seemed like the open farm girl she was. After being ignored, if not openly rebuffed, she became a quieter person. "My husband said not to

**53**

★                                    ★                                    ★

worry. The wives would call me for my first coffee." But only her mother called.

Even if wives had called, Emily would have been the newcomer, the outsider, who would have had to have the guts to "tough it out" until they made room for her in the established friendships of the tight-knit group of wives. The most she could have expected was a call asking her to the wives' first coffee. If she had gone, she would have had to take the initiative to make friends. Until time eased her into a friendship or she found a job to help pass the time, she would have had to deal with feelings that threatened to overwhelm her this first time away from home. Emily felt as alone and invisible as a bag lady on a teeming city street.

This first time alone as a Navy wife tested her mettle. It forced her to rely on her own resources, to grow up quickly, and so discover that she had the guts to go it alone. She had nights that were sleepless with yearning, cuddling her husband's pillow, soaking it with her tears. She experienced pangs of loneliness, even in a group. Some mornings she didn't want to get up. And when her mother did call, it was hard to sound cheerful. But she tried. The military would have frowned on Emily complaining. Wives were expected *not* to complain. Even senior wives expected this of junior wives.

How many weeks and months does the military wife have to survive by herself? Emily is not the only military wife to have struggled alone in a strange place—and she won't be the last. Loneliness is a condition of military marriages even for the strongest. When a woman marries a military man, she contracts to a marriage in which the abnormal is accepted as the norm. She may live without her husband more than fifty percent of her married life, though she is never fully prepared for him to leave. She knows that a Navy career means long stretches at sea, but until she lives empty months by herself, far removed from her family and friends, she won't fully comprehend how debilitating being alone can be.

Perhaps more than anything else, it is her ability to survive alone

★　　　　　　　　　★　　　　　　　　　★

that so dramatically sets the military wife apart from her civilian sister. If she survives, the young military wife like Emily tends to mature faster, to be stronger, more of a take-charge person, more resilient to change. She becomes her own person. Because of her travels to exotic ports, she leads a more adventuresome life than her civilian counterpart who marries a hometown boy and settles nearby, nurtured by family and friends. Even if the civilian has a job that requires extensive travel, the quality of that separation is quite different from that experienced by a military couple. When a military wife says goodbye to her husband, not only will she not see him for months at a time, she may not be able to communicate with him in an emergency. Emily could write to her husband but his ship was deployed in a war zone and getting shot at, so weeks might pass before she got a reply. Each time her husband left, she had to work through grief that psychologists have said is as intense as that experienced by new widows.

A survey of Navy wives conducted by the Norfolk *Virginian-Pilot* confirmed that "by far the greatest fear is that their men will not return alive: 53 percent of the survey respondents cited the danger of their husbands' jobs and the possibility of combat. War, they point out, and its modern extension, terrorism, have an immediacy for a military wife that her civilian counterparts cannot imagine."

### RARELY NINE TO FIVE

The military couple, as Emily learned, sacrifices time and togetherness. A military man is often deployed. Even when he is stationed at home, the needs of the military keep him away. There are TDY assignments (temporary duty) for three to six months. Since it is temporary, wife and family stay behind. "Remotes" can separate the military man from his wife and family for a year or more. He can be sent unaccompanied to any isolated spot on the globe such as Korea, Iceland, Saudi Arabia, or Diego Garcia, (a tiny island in the Indian Ocean). Destroyers and submarines are sent on weekly operations and/or long cruises of six to nine months. Marines deploy on extended "floats" for training and maneuvers. The Army deploys soldiers "in the field" anywhere from a few weeks to several months. Flying times differ for Air Force personnel, but the hours are long and the separations are many.

How many civilians realize that at least once a month a Strategic Air Command flight crew "stands alert"—restricted to base and required to live at the alert pad, apart from their families? The SAC mission is operational readiness, being able to put the plane in the air at a moment's notice. Even though their families may live in base housing just blocks from the facility, the crew might as well be out of state for all the good it does the families. One wife at a Strategic Air Command base in Rapid City, South Dakota, was angry that a family emergency couldn't bring her husband home the afternoon her son broke his arm. "I called my husband for help. They put me through to him right away but there was no way he could even get off alert to take us to the Emergency Room. So I had a neighbor take me. He finally met us there, but, boy, was I pissed."

Being on alert and unable to get away to help in a crisis at home may sound irrational to a worried mother, but to the SAC people nothing can stand in the way of readiness. They are playing "for real." Someday, they rationalize, the alert will not be just a readiness game and a son's broken arm cannot stand in the way of military needs.

In between assignments away from home base, all services rotate the men to shore duty or home-based assignments, but the hours never seem to be nine to five and the weekends may not belong exclusively to the family. Some men are "on call" and as such come home with a beeper. Others must stay home within reach of a phone. All servicemen stand the duty, which often is working around the clock at a command post on the base, after completing normal working hours. This duty section is essentially on alert for any incoming messages or crises that need to be handled. The cycle of standing the

★                              ★                              ★

duty may be as frequent as every other day, or it could be one day of duty in three working days, or once a month depending on the duty roster. Even if he is not standing the duty, if the military man is on a seagoing vessel or a flight crew, he stays on the job until it is completed—no matter how long it takes—cutting into his time at home with the family.

The senior enlisted and officers may not stand duty as often as the younger men, but their work hours may be longer because of responsibilities. Even though there is no overtime pay in service, the military makes an effort to see that the men receive "comp time," when the work load decreases. But somehow it never seems enough to make up for the time they've lost—time most civilians enjoy with their families on a regular basis.

It is obvious with all the separations that not all women have the constitution to be military wives. First of all, they must be flexible enough to survive the turmoil caused by their husbands' constant comings and goings. They must deal with the stresses of two radically different life-styles: on the one hand as a celibate, single parent living alone when her husband is gone; on the other as a lover/wife/mother/ hostess when he is home.

If the husband is frequently gone, then even the at-home times are far from normal. Just as a roller coaster plummets its riders from exhilarating highs to stomach-clutching lows, the military wife is locked into the emotional ride for the duration of her husband's time in the service. The wife experiences extraordinary upheavals as she constantly makes adjustments to her husband's schedule. She moves at a moment's notice, giving up her job, status in the community, and a newly established network of friends. It is the military way of life and wives put up with it because they feel they are doing their patriotic duty. So many of the wives interviewed did not perceive that they had a choice or that they could control their lives. Either they got off the roller coaster by divorcing, or the men got out of the service. Or they survived by not quite loving their men so much.

★ ★ ★

Imagine how precious are the days and hours allotted to military couples as husband and wife. As the time is shortened, they will spend as much of their time together as they possibly can. They will socialize with other couples in the same environment, go out to dinner and movies by themselves. During this time emotional highs are intensified. They honeymoon and become reacquainted.

When her husband is home, the wife structures her time around him, observes Alice Snyder, Ph.D., who studied families of submariners for her doctoral thesis, *Separations and Reunions: Their Impact on the Submariner's Wife*. Meals also become more formalized, with the family sitting around the table. When the husband is gone, the wife and kids grab quick fast-food meals. She is the one the children turn to for all their needs. When he comes home, she makes room for Daddy in their lives. It takes a strong couple with good communication skills to work through these trying times of transition.

It not only takes good communication skills, it takes a strong woman with good coping skills, with either a career, studies that absorb her time, or children to rear. It seems that the woman most vulnerable during separations is the newlywed barely out of high school, alone for the first time without any options to fill her time. How she manages during that first separation sets the pattern for her future. If the marriage is to remain viable, the military wife must learn to survive alone, growing stronger as obstacles are overcome and keeping the lines of communication open.

In some instances, there are classes to help military wives learn to cope with separation. The military has established programs to assist families. However, as one health care professional pointed out, the name "family service program" is misleading. The programs serve the military—not the family. The programs exist to keep the wife/family functioning in the context of the military so that the military member can give his all to Uncle Sam without worrying about his family. As examples of the kind of help a wife can find, one Navy family service

★                    ★                    ★

center offers classes on "Coping with Stress," "Post Deployment Blues," and "Money Management"—not lessons in lobbying the government to shorten submarine patrols or moving families less often or even keeping the destroyers anchored at home.

Wives are constantly reminded of how important their supportive role is. On Okinawa, Armed Services television consistently runs "commercials" telling wives how they must cope with their husbands' return, assuring them not to be anxious about the reunion, that everything will work out, that *they* must be patient.

But what happens when the wives become too strong and too independent? Several wives interviewed told how they had grown from being very dependent, bowing to their husbands' wishes, hardly able to wait for them to come home, to becoming totally take-charge people.

"I learned that I could survive without him," noted a Navy chief's wife. "It started with a really good job that got me out with people. When his patrol was over, I wasn't ready for him to come home because I knew he would upset everything. He expected me to quit my job and be there for him twenty-four hours a day. He was furious when I told him no. For a few months I was sure our marriage was over. I was ready to just walk out on this whole life. He gradually came to realize that I could not stay within four walls. I would have been a nut case in a short while. We had to compromise—both of us—to keep our marriage together."

The bottom line is simply this: the military must be operational. Ships are going to sail; planes must be in the air. The military views the woman's main job as supporting her husband and this military bureaucracy. She is to suffer in silence, and not rock the boat. The question remains: is marriage compatible with a military career? The all-volunteer military is facing acute manpower shortages because many couples are saying no. Those who choose to stay in and serve Uncle Sam are doing so at great personal sacrifice.

**59**

★                              ★                              ★

## Throwing Mama From the Train

A military wife not only loses her husband to frequent separations, she loses the closeness of her mother, her family, and friends—all that is familiar. And each move takes her away from new-found friends. Being a military wife might not be as difficult if she were with her family while he was gone. However, it is rare for a woman to marry a military man and then stay in her hometown, although if her hometown is near a major military base, she may one day return.

A given fact of a military marriage is a nomadic life. Each time a military wife moves it is like experiencing a loved one's death, says Suzanne Burris, Army wife and certified marriage and family therapist. "Each move is a loss, and you must go through a grieving period for the loss before you can move ahead. There are all kinds of losses involved in moving: relationships, jobs, friends, home, and family. Each loss brings up all past losses and—unless dealt with—can cause major problems. Even if the grieving is mild and only labeled homesickness it must be faced."

One young woman of twenty-three called it homesickness. She sat cross-legged in a neatly pressed T-shirt and jeans in her pleasantly furnished duplex. They were newlyweds when his orders moved him from San Diego to Charleston, South Carolina. "My husband, who was a first class petty officer (E-6) when we married, was home only two weeks in Charleston before he left for a three-month patrol on a nuclear-powered submarine. Once he left, I couldn't phone him. For a month we could write, but after he was submerged, he was out of touch for sixty days. I was three thousands miles away from my family's annual Christmas dinner in San Diego. The relatives were all good about calling me, but the calls made me feel even more lonely. Some other wives from the submarine invited me to dinner, which helped pass the time. But they were still strangers—not family—and I was really hurting that first holiday alone."

Readjustment takes time. Most wives say it takes six to eight months

★                           ★                           ★

before they feel comfortable in new surroundings. With each move, a woman leaves behind her identity, her "specialness," the achievements that make her an individual. If she is to go on, she must begin to reconnect with all that is important to her. If she is an artist, she begins creating and marketing herself and her paintings once again. If she loves doing crafts, she finds a class. Jeanette, a highly skilled hospital worker advised, "If you work, you need to immediately start looking for a job because when you move you have to get yourself adjusted into your normal life-style as quickly as you can. You are not going to start to meet people or get into your normal life pattern until you have a job."

A vital part of the readjustment, say many wives, is to allow time to grieve for all that has been left behind. Even when the frequency of military moves gives her little time to grieve, it's important to recognize that sadness is part of the whole recovery process.

Marianne, a Navy wife in her thirties, was bright enough to know she had to give herself time to adjust to her new location. She offered coffee as she sat in her sparkling clean house. "I didn't want to come to San Diego—neither did my two boys. We were happy in Hawaii. I had just broken through the years of substitute teaching and had my first real job offer teaching math in a private school. When we moved here, our first eight months were horrendous. One son hated his school, and his grades started to show it. I had to start all over again making friends. It's hard, let me tell you. It seemed once I got settled and found a job I really liked, we began to feel this place was home."

The key seems to be making friends who serve as substitutes for close family ties. Older women may serve as mother figures but, more important, they serve as sisters, forming bonds, helping each other out by just being there during times of extraordinary stress.

## THE SISTERHOOD

To help regain a sense of belonging, bonding occurs between women. Sometimes it lasts only for the time the men are gone, but often it blossoms into lifelong friendships continued long distance when the women move apart. It happens most often among women of small commands such as flight crews or submarines.

"There is a sisterhood on submarines," explained a Navy lieutenant's wife interviewed during her lunch break at a bustling restaurant. "It is a community, a microcosm within itself. Within that system there is always someone you can call on for information such as the most sympathetic doctor, or for help with appliance repair, or even the best place in town to buy good yarn." She put down her fork, thought for a moment, and then said, "In the old days there wasn't an existing social work organization and life really had to get out of hand before you got help. My mentor was a chief's wife who was like my big sister. She told me not only how to live as a Navy wife but gave me a really positive attitude about being a service wife. Now there is an ombudsman program, an official system of volunteers trained by the Navy family service personnel to assist other Navy wives with information and referrals to agencies for help if needed. These volunteers serve as the official liaison between the ship and the wives."

Another wife, who married an ensign, found it difficult to live through the separations, "which are definitely long and frequent. When you are away from your home, then you start to realize what family really means even as you discover you can live without them. However, if you are wise, you start to develop friendships and rapport with women in the submarine community because they are going to be your lifeline when your husband leaves. Because submarines are deployed at different times, you find yourself in some pretty strange friendships that are based on the understanding that if your husband is gone and hers is home, you don't bother them. Their time together is precious, so your friendship with that woman is put on hold until he leaves. It is good to be friendly with the wives on your boat because they are going to be available for you when you need someone."

Having other wives in the same situation provides a networking system for the new wife. As a destroyer wife said, "When I moved, it

★                              ★                              ★

was often after the destroyer had deployed. You have no opportunity to meet someone for social interaction; you're depressed, lonely. We had our wardroom wives on the destroyer as well as the Destroyers Officers' Wives' Club. None of them helped at first when I was a newcomer. You have to start cold. Even when you are happy or thrilled over an event, you have no one to tell it to, no one to go shopping with. Or you're pregnant for the first time in your life and you don't have your mother to tell you feeling blue or being sick to your stomach is natural. If you are with someone who can tell you all of those feelings are perfectly natural, it is a big help. When you are far from your family, it is just natural that you reach out to other Navy wives to help out. I now have skills in doing that because having had to cope for so long, I had to learn them; they didn't come naturally."

## THE LONELY C.O.W.'S

As husbands progress up the ladder, it doesn't get easier. It gets lonelier. The sisterhood of "lower" ranking wives gets left behind. And, conversely, many C.O.W.'s (Commanding Officers' Wives) say their husbands' promotions led to their being dropped by friends. However, in spite of the hardships, these wives choose to stick it out because, they say, they feel "in sync" with military life, they love the socializing, the money, the power. (For an idea of how much money, see Appendix.) They knowingly sacrifice companionship for the loneliness of living with a man who is a workaholic, a man driven to achieve the highest command.

"I think we put up with more as Navy wives than we would married to a man who worked for the telephone company all of his life. More is asked of me than I would be giving as the wife of a civilian," noted Lynda, a commanding officer's wife. She was alone in her large house. Her husband had been gone for two months. Before the interview was over, the quiet was shattered by the arrival of her teenagers home from school. "Certainly, with us being in the service, it has been

★                              ★                              ★

more exciting and given me a chance to go places and meet people I never would have if I had stayed and married someone from National Cash Register. The Navy gets a lot from me, a lot of work, a lot of volunteer time. When the problems of being a C.O.'s wife get to be too much, I can either talk to another commander's wife or to a counselor who is bound by oath not to reveal what is said. Sometimes it is terribly lonely. As far as I was concerned, I was just another wife, so I was not prepared for this break from the other wives when my husband became an X.O. [executive officer]. That division between me and the other wives was really complete when he made C.O. because it seemed to me that I began to be excluded from some of the wives' gatherings. . . . However, when I became aware that the younger officers' wives were having socials and didn't invite me, it really hurt my feelings. If two of them went out to lunch, that's different, but when all of them went out . . . that really hurt. I guess they feel inhibited because now I'm a commander's wife."

Having to face a lifetime of being alone, of solving all of life's problems by yourself, comes with the territory of marrying an ambitious man in the military.

Caroline, an admiral's wife, was interviewed in spacious quarters set high on a hill in senior officers' housing. The ticking of a grandfather clock subtly punctuated the quiet. She was a no-nonsense woman, helpful yet obviously used to leading people. She explained: "My husband has spent all of his Navy career in destroyers. Their operating schedule was such that he was gone a great deal of time out to sea. Even when he was in port, the men were all working such terrible hours to get ready for various performance, operational, and material tests that I never saw him, and other wives did not see a great deal of their husbands. The stresses put on the family and wives in many cases were difficult to deal with by oneself.

"One of the biggest differences between the civilian and military is the wife does not have to deal with the stresses alone [in military life]. When the military husband is gone, there is the bonding between

★                                    ★                                    ★

wives. At all of the seagoing commands my husband had, I felt it was important to give the new wives a focal point to their lives and have opportunities to meet others in the same position. Within each command, we formed a small community of wives, even though each command was different in the size of the ship and the makeup of the group. Some wives' groups had close interaction between enlisted and officers' wives. Some groups were more social than others; some offered more family activities.

"As my husband became more senior, the ships under his command became bigger and the wardroom larger. As that occurred, I became less able to deal with the large numbers [and I could not] become personally involved with all the wives on the ship. It became more important to me to set up support groups for the enlisted and the officers' wives. It was not a conscious effort to divide the wives, but more of a conscious effort to see that they were all taken care of. I say taken care of, because up to just a few years ago, there was no family service center or ombudsman program to help the wives and families when the ship was deployed. If there was a family emergency in which the mother had to spend her time with a youngster in the hospital, then someone had to feed and clothe the children left at home. It was important to have a system to take care of problems such as this. Back then, such a system was totally informal and some were more effective than others."

A destroyer is a seagoing vessel. During one two-year tour, the destroyer Caroline's husband commanded was gone on a nine-month trip away from the home port. When in the home port the crew still went out for daily operations or for monthly operations for three weeks at a time. When they were in, most of the crew stood "one-in-threes," which meant they worked a normal workday and then stood a twenty-four-hour duty aboard the ship followed by two nights at home.

Women like Caroline are not anomalies in the military. What is unique about her is that as she moved to the top with her husband,

★ ★ ★

she looked around her to see what needed to be done. Then she inaugurated the networking and wives' groups that she saw a need to establish. Without women like her, the wife at the bottom would more than likely be left to survive on her own. As it is, too many women are not getting included in lifesaving networks.

## IT'S LONELIER OVERSEAS

Wives moving from base to base within the continental United States may find a need for such a network different from that of those wives sent overseas. Even if the husband is home there is a new culture overseas and a new way of life to get used to. For the first time a wife realizes she is the outsider and must make the effort to learn the language and the culture. One of two things seems to happen: either the wife considers her life an adventure and starts exploring her new land, or she withdraws into the "safety" of the base compound. If her husband travels frequently from the overseas base, her loneliness seems magnified because of the distance to her family.

"All I wanted was a hug. It was so lonely in Japan when my husband was flying. I missed him, I missed having someone to sleep with at night, I missed having him around," explained Kathy, a vivacious black woman married to a Navy pilot of a P-3 Orion, a submarine patrol aircraft. "You get tired of talking to a twelve-year-old. There were times all I wanted was a warm hug. We wives used to laugh together about our chaplain. We told him we'd pay him a dollar a hug," she laughed. "Boy, did he give good hugs! Yet, you know what?" she asked, looking up with a grin. "I didn't dare hug another husband. I would have incurred the wrath of jealous wives and been accused of trying to steal their husbands. It was hands off!

"Yet if we needed any other kind of help it was always there. We had a duty husband," Kathy went on to explain. "He was the one we could call on to help fix our car or the TV. But you'd never think of hugging him." She paused for a moment. "You know I realized that the loneliness I experienced depended on where we were stationed. I

★         ★         ★

experienced a different kind of lonely—it was more bearable—when we were living on the East Coast near my family. Cameron was gone, I missed him, and I was lonely but not as lonely, because my family was close by to give me hugs and the close contact I needed."

Loneliness is compounded when the husband leaves, and most social activities cease until he returns. The usual pattern is to socialize nonstop while the husband is home. There are many functions for couples that stop dead the moment the husband leaves. That's why the wives' groups are a help, noted Lila, a Navy chief's wife. "One good example was the informal wives' group at Vallejo, California. I had never been away from home before but it seemed that everyone just banded together when the husbands left. There were a lot of wives' functions; we went out for luncheons and dinners when our husbands were gone. It would be real casual—someone would just decide where we were going for dinner and we'd have to call in by a certain date. Then we'd decide who was going to drive and who would be riding with whom. The only time a get-together was formal was when the captain's wife had tea for all of us."

"With the men TDY so much now from Ellsworth Air Force Base, we lead such separate lives here in Rapid City," said Ann, wife of an Air Force pilot. "My husband is gone a great part of each month and I feel alienated and sometimes I'm made to feel guilty. I have male friends from the bank where I work and occasionally I go to the movies or have dinner after work. One night a friend of ours came through and spent the night in the guest room. The next morning when the phone rang he answered. It was another Air Force wife calling, and she said to me later: 'Was that your husband I got on the telephone the other day?' I didn't lie. I told her it was my friend. I'm sure she was rather upset. I'm always afraid that people will say things. I'm not sure Steve is comfortable about my other relationships, but I tell him, 'I'm living in South Dakota for you.' "

Another officer's wife said, "I give dinner parties even when my husband is gone. Why should I deprive myself of stimulating conver-

★                              ★                              ★

sation?" When she needed an escort she called on a friend. "He was a friend of mine, and you might also say a friend of my husband. When my husband is home he comes over for dinner."

Then there are the husbands who attempt to control their wives— even when they are gone. Some husbands tell wives they have to stay home while the husbands are gone. "I remember one wife whose husband told her she could only drive her car to the commissary and to the hospital," explained Lila. "She called me up and told me in that little-girl voice of hers that George would get mad at her if she took the car anywhere else." Ellen, the ex-wife of a Marine sergeant, mentioned the severe restrictions her husband placed on her as a major factor contributing to her divorce. "When we were at this small Marine site in the California mountains he would take the car keys to work with him, even if he was going to be gone several days, so that I could not leave home while he was away. I was stuck in a small trailer all day, waiting until he came to drive me to the cleaners or grocery shopping. Of course, I was very young and a new bride, so it took me a while before I decided I simply couldn't live as his prisoner." Social workers became involved in an extreme case involving a wife left starving because the husband had taken the wife's military I.D. card, effectively cutting her off from shopping on the base and from social contacts.

## WHEN HUGS AREN'T ENOUGH

With all the support from other wives that is available, marriage to a military man is still a lonely life. And not all women survive. Some discover by the end of the first separation that they simply cannot live alone and they return home. Others have simply said to their husbands, 'It's either me or the service.' The military does not retain statistics on the number of divorces; however, one chaplain interviewed said the number of divorced military couples was as high, if not higher, than civilians. In addition to the divorced and those who

★                    ★                    ★

return home, there is yet another type of wife who should never be left alone—those who are deeply troubled.

"As young as I was, it soon became obvious to me that one of our wardroom wives was—for want of better words—a mental case. I am not mincing words. Here was a woman who should not have been left alone, who needed competent medical help and was not getting it, and I don't know why," explained Anne, a commander's wife, choosing her words with great care. She lit up a cigarette before continuing. "I worried about her, for I recognized in her the same symptoms of a friend of mine. I talked to this woman's husband, asking him to make an appointment for her with a psychiatrist before he left for sea duty. It was becoming obvious that the situation was becoming serious and I was afraid for her. At the same time there was a growing reluctance on the part of the other wives to be around her because she had started to act so crazy. The submarine left on its patrol—they were always leaving on patrols—and I knew she had this appointment with the psychiatrist. A couple of days went by and because I hadn't heard from her, I called the captain's wife and told her of my concern. She insisted I not go by myself, because she was afraid the other wife might be dangerous. So the X.O.'s wife went with me." Pausing, she inhaled. In a slow, quiet voice she said, "It was quite a mess. The woman had shot herself several days before and was shut up in the house. I had to break in. . . ." She stopped to compose herself.

"I can't ever quit thinking about that wife. She made such an impression on me. I felt so much guilt for so long afterward. If only I had stayed with her, or insisted she go into the hospital. But I didn't. I'm helping with a similar problem right now. Obviously, she needs help, but she has to decide to get that help on her own: no one can step in and force her. If children are being abused or neglected, then the authorities use that as a lever to help. There are some poor souls who are never going to get used to their husbands leaving them. This gal who killed herself was one of them. She was mentally ill. It's made me more aware of similar problems with other wives."

There are women who don't survive as military wives, or else survive but at great personal loss. While the numbers of women who take their own lives are at a minimum, there is no doubt that separations and loneliness exacerbate existing mental health problems. Depression, feelings of inadequacy, and alienation run through the conversations of many of the wives. Is it just that they view themselves as victims of the system, or have they endured one too many rides on the roller coaster that have broken down their resources?

The answer is simply that it differs from woman to woman. What it boils down to is that the life of a military wife is a test of her inner strengths and resources. Many wives say they make an appointment to see a base doctor because "something" is wrong. Each invariably says that once the military doctor uncovers the fact her husband is deployed, he does not take her seriously. The lucky women are the ones who find competent psychological care to help them through serious depression.

"There is a lot of anger that builds up because of all of the denial of the wife's feelings if she is going to function as a 'good' wife," explained Priscilla Gates, M.E.d. (Masters in Education), a child, marriage, and family counselor, interviewed in her office near two large military complexes in Hawaii. "All of that time takes its toll. Often the wife can't articulate why she is feeling depressed. How can you say you are mad as hell because your husband has deserted you, that you can't communicate with him? All of the other wives not only defend the job the husbands are doing but preach that one should keep a stiff upper lip. There's even the little voice inside of each that says he didn't leave to pursue his own pleasure and how can you think of burdening him further with what you are going through? Over the course of the years, all of this built-up anger often leads to depression, and it is usually the wife who comes in for help or professional counseling."

★        ★        ★

Another care-giver would say that counseling should be provided not just for the sake of wives, but for the sake of the military. Constantine J. G. Cretekos, a psychiatrist, stated in an article in *Military Medicine* that not enough attention has been paid to the soldier's wife and her problems. "Situated in a pivotal position, she may aid her husband in withstanding military pressures, or encourage him to succumb to those pressures. She plays a crucial role in fulfilling the military mission: to preserve the fighting strength," notes Dr. Cretekos. "Her ability to weather separation allows her husband to fulfill his military obligation. If she collapses, this may necessitate the serviceman's return home to give her assistance. The soldier and his wife form a dynamic dyad. An understanding of the one necessitates examining the other."

Most wives give lip service to that old saying the needs of the service always come before the needs of the family. However, among the wives interviewed who no longer felt the needs of the service came first in their lives was one officer's wife who clearly saw she did not want to continue living alone, then uprooting time and time again. She and her husband were stationed at an Army post for three years. That was long enough to buy and settle into the community. Orders came that assigned him to a post a couple of hundred of miles away— too far for commuting. There was a year's wait for housing. They decided to tough it out. He commuted home on weekends. After a year, even though there was a slot open for him at his old base, and his boss endorsed his transfer, the Army did not choose to return him. He resigned his commission as a major. If he had stayed in the Army his wife would have been raising their two teenage boys alone for more than two years. In her mind, the reasons for getting out were overwhelming, and they stretched over the years.

"I remember vignettes of times I had to manage by myself," Colleen said in a matter-of-fact tone that for a while held in check her anger and sadness. She sat in her comfortable home, watching her boys frolic in their pool, with a contented cat on her lap. "I was *so* lonely.

**71**

I longed for friends and my home in Washington state. I remember being twenty-three. My husband was in Korea. We were supposed to move from Fort Lewis [Washington] to Georgia when he came back. I was supposed to make the arrangements. My car was broken and a friend drove me to the fort from Tacoma. I waited through a class on military benefits at the end of which I got papers to fill out. I stood in lines for a couple of hours. Then, at the end, [the papers] could not be processed because they did not have my husband's orders. I remember a cold, solemn hall, and gray walls that supported me as I leaned against them, holding my eleven-month-old son, who never knew his father. A young soldier came out of a room and asked me what was wrong, and I explained I couldn't complete my task, or even start it, because I didn't have my husband's orders. He happened to be a records clerk who expedited everything," she said with a wry smile at how things worked out.

"I remember days, months, years alone. I remember never getting too close because he would leave. Always strong, always alone. Always cheer him up because at least you're home in civilization with the kids and he's off God knows where in danger and I'm worried about bills, chicken pox, the broken water heater, plugged pipes, dead car, the pregnant cat—and him.

"There is nothing left for me, now that I'm thirty-five instead of twenty-three. Nothing is left except bitterness. When I drive on an Army base my blood runs cold. When I see an officer I want to stomp on his shiny shoes. The Army is not a way of life. It destroys people. It destroys relationships. It makes men into megalomaniacs who see only the next step on the ladder of success. They don't care about their wives or their families. It's a big game they play, though—they always commend those same wives and children for their sacrifices they have made. I have made too many sacrifices."

There is no neat closure on an interview brimming with so much anger. How can you walk in someone's shoes until you realize she recently sat for hours comforting a wife whose husband was acciden-

★       ★       ★

tally shot by his own troops—not in a war zone, but as they were playing war games with real bullets on United States soil at the Army's National Training Center in the California desert. Life as civilians has its own problems, yet Colleen and her husband have made the transition. They are active, productive people in their community, making the time for their children and each other. This means leading a far more normal life as a married couple away from the overriding control and the male machismo that permeate Uncle Sam's company towns.

★          ★          ★

If the Navy had wanted you to have a wife they would have issued you one with your seabag.

—OLD NAVY SAYING

★                              ★                              ★

Tightly gripping the handles, Marianne steered the stroller on a fixed course straight down the pier to the distant gangplank leading to her husband's ship. As a solitary woman awash in a sea of sailors, she was at once uncomfortable and exhilarated. She felt the sailors' eyes and heard their whistles as she passed resolutely through their midst, face flushed not only from the fast pace but from the heightened awareness of being a woman and as out of place as a robed nun in a nudist colony.

Step foot on a military base and a female encounters this male bastion, relatively untouched by either military wives or female military members. A wife will repeatedly hear the male adage: "If the Navy wanted you to have a wife they would have issued you one with your seabag." She sees bumper stickers with sexual double entendres: "Submariners have bigger balls" (for the annual submarine birthday ball), "Submariners do it deeper," "The Marines last longer," and "The Air Force does it with precision," and so on.

The sum of all she sees and hears makes her wonder just what place a woman does have on a military base. Is she only a camp follower after years of being a wife? Does she only exist to pander to male hormones, comfort the warrior for his short stay at home, and then wait patiently for his return? Although simplistic, it seems from their actions as if the military views the wife in a stereotypical way as either a readily available female/whore or a nun, carefully cloistered in club activities until the husband returns. Even the female military member fares no better. Will she ever be recognized as a woman doing her job when wives see her as a threat and men view her as an opportunity?

**75**

More females are serving side by side with men—worry enough for the wives—but they also bunk with men (in separate rooms) during Air Force SAC crew alerts and on select Navy oceangoing ships in all-female quarters.

Stereotypes paint with a broad brush and are inaccurate. Obviously, not all military men are womanizers; not all military wives play around. Most military couples have found ways to forge strong marriages—in spite of the atmosphere of promiscuity that surrounds the military. Long separations, loneliness, anonymity in far-flung ports make sexual encounters relatively easy when compared to those in small busybody towns. Of course, a civilian businessman can travel to a distant city and buy himself a night of fun. Of course, a woman can find a man to help her pass the time alone. It happens with civilians; it happens with military. Infidelity is a real factor. Casual sex is an option some choose. There is no figure kept of how many military partners stray—at least as many as in the civilian sector, say some; others say much higher. Divorces number as high, if not higher, in military marriages as in civilian marriages.

What's it like being married to a military man? It is building a marriage and open communication with someone who is gone more than half the time. It means trusting him when he enters the world of Suzy Wong overseas. It means trying to maintain a life that has the highs of honeymoons followed by bottoming out when he leaves. It means acknowledging the stresses of a sexual being leading a celibate life while he is gone. It means not having the anchor of an extended family to fall back on during long periods of time alone. It means growing into a strong human being who somehow weathers the storms.

The military doesn't make it any easier. Since little is being done to end prostitution around military bases, it would seem the military condones prostitutes, massage parlors, and "temporary wives" for the good of the military man and ultimately the good of the military.

★ ★ ★

## THE MILITARY AND THE "MASSAGE" PARLORS

Wives interviewed angrily complained about the availability of casual sex, especially overseas.

"The stories I hear from the Philippines are enough to curl your hair," said Angela, an elegant, titian-haired woman. She sat in her comfortably furnished base quarters sipping Perrier and lime. "Maybe the AIDS scare will slow down business in 'liberty' ports. It used to be that the wives would say, 'As long as I don't know about it, his fling won't hurt me.' Now, none of us are sure. It's no longer V.D. that's the worry. It's the possibility of us *dying*. At one of our last coffees before the flight crew got back, we got talking about AIDS. Several of us thought that the military condones extramarital affairs because it has not cleaned up massage parlors, houses of prostitution, or restricted activities of bar girls who work as prostitutes outside the bases. The United States government overseas even monitors the health of the local prostitutes, which, in our opinion, implies complicity. One Air Force wife was told that in Thailand and Vietnam the 'girls' had numbers. Each week they were checked for venereal disease and if they were safe, their number was read over the base radio. Commanders in the area obviously looked the other way, for the practice was allowed to continue. When our men were first sent to these areas overseas they were cautioned to carefully read the girl's identification card to insure that the picture was of the woman, not a 'safe' card she borrowed to stay in business.

"Vietnam was a rough time for us wives, not only because of the very real dangers of our husbands being in a war zone but because of the stories coming back to us," Angela continued. "Prostitutes were so available. We became aware of the fact that in Thailand and the Philippines the government closely monitored prostitutes to keep them free of disease, so the guys felt fairly comfortable about not bringing something home. I remember my husband telling me that when he was in Taiwan, billeted in government-contracted hotels off

**77**

base, a massage girl willing to service him came with the room. Some were blind girls who earned their living by giving massages. Others were available for more intimate services. In Thailand, these temporary liaisons were informally contracted, a 'wife', for the duration of his assignment. In Okinawa the 'steam and cream' parlors offered every imaginable sexual service.

"It was awfully good for the guys," Angela continued in angry, clipped words, "for they had absolutely no responsibility to the family, beyond providing that monthly allotment. We were left trying to keep the kids, the house, and the yard up to the standards of the base commander. We were expected to stay home and maintain. I saw a lot of divorces during the time of Vietnam, an awful lot."

Among the wives, Korea is thought of in one of two ways: either as a great shopping destination or as a heartache for the wives left at home because of the way the Korean women pamper American men. Even if a wife is in Korea with her husband—and many are not because some assignments along the DMZ in Korea are considered remote tours to which the man is sent alone—they are left at home for many social engagements. Young and beautiful single women are assigned to each man by the host. After dinner the women are often available. Korea continues to be a place where the military man can arrange to have a *jo-san*, or a temporary live-in "wife."

"I think it is rare that you found a man who hated to be in Korea," said an Army colonel's wife. "Many military orders were for an unaccompanied tour, which meant he could leave the problems of wife and family behind. The minute he got orders the other guys in the office would tell him how much he was going to love it. Why shouldn't he? It's a great place for a guy to be stationed unless he is up at the DMZ and out of the action. But if he is in any town, he is totally welcomed. The Koreans have lots of coffeehouses with plenty of young ladies, and the men are free to make their own arrangements. Everyone looks the other way. It may not be the official position, but no one is stopping it. In fact, they can invite these women back on

\*     \*     \*

post for dinner or to their quarters and it is just thought: 'Oh, those poor guys are lonely and they are far from their families.' And can you imagine the trouble a wife has trying to compete with a relationship in Shangri-la? After having a year of some honey taking care of his every need with no responsibilities of wife or family, the man has a hard time fitting back in, as does the wife who has to contend with what might have gone on."

Korea and the Far East are not the only coveted assignments. Most overseas destinations in Europe mean the "old boy" network in Europe will provide "companionship" to visiting officers. As one colonel's wife explained: "In our early tours, especially in Italy, I was very much aware of officers on TDY assignments who were taken to the best places for dinner and entertainment. If the visitors desired to have a woman it could be arranged, very discreetly by a wink and a nudge, with key phrases such as 'Do you want a little extra?' Providing the girls was thought of as an amenity, a way to make your place look a little better, make the VIP's trip a little more memorable, and make them remember you at promotion time."

## THE MILITARY HOUSES OF PROSTITUTION

None of these "extras" are new. Houses of prostitution and red-light districts have historically operated near military bases. But there was only one city in which prostitution operated legally: Honolulu.

During World War II, Honolulu was the only city with a population of more than one hundred thousand that not only tolerated but encouraged open houses of prostitution. Most American moviegoing audiences remember only hints of such illicit action after censors finished cutting the film *The Revolt of Mamie Stover*. A *Time* magazine review said: "Part fiction and part fact, the book [by William Bradford Huie] recounted the life of a woman who invented a sort of assembly-line method of servicing the servicemen in Honolulu during World War II."

During the war years, brothels operated legally and openly under martial law, which usurped the powers of the territorial government of Hawaii. Interestingly, the operation of the twenty houses (with two hundred and fifty women registered as prostitutes) was so profitable that prostitution was allowed to continue until near the end of the war. The established rates, of three dollars to five dollars for three minutes with a prostitute, netted big money—an estimated annual gross income of fifteen million dollars. While the subject of allowing prostitution to continue was hotly debated in the community at the time, it is ironic that it was only *after* the troops began to return home that community-minded citizens surfaced to force closure of the houses on September 21, 1944, by the police commission. Even then debate raged not because of the moral question as much as the tremendous loss of legal revenue.

To enable prostitution to prosper during the war years apparently meant a collusion between the territorial government and the military. War Depository records, now yellowed and fragile with age, don't spell out a direct order allowing houses of prostitution; however, references included in Section I, General Orders No. 107, show that the military and civilian governments worked hand in hand. Major Laurence J. Stuppy, medical corps, medical service, Central Pacific Base Command, reported on the low rate of venereal disease in servicemen, which he said was due to the "close, energetic teamwork between services and the territorial board of health in the detection, isolation, and treatment of the human sources of infection."

Section I, General Orders No. 107, from the office of the military governor, concerns the control of communicable disease and laws. During the time of military rule, the Army program for control of communicable disease included a three-point plan:

1. Regulations were in place that every six months all troops would hear a talk on sex hygiene;
2. There would be adequate prophylactic facilities, and both individual and dispensary care provided;

*                              *                              *

3. Troops were inspected for disease monthly and semimonthly.

The presence of the brothels was further justified by many as "saving" decent women from potential rape. Riley H. Allen in *The Fight on Prostitution Has Just Begun*, noted that the "presence here of hundreds of thousands of members of the armed forces and war workers puts the community under special pressure and in the minds of many men makes it necessary to have an 'outlet' in the form of houses of prostitution. This is the basis for 'soldiers and sailors must have women, and Honolulu should provide them.' "

J. Garner Anthony, a well-known Honolulu judge of his time, described how the military controlled the local press so that no reference to prostitution surfaced in the Honolulu newspapers during the war years. Anthony writes in his book, *Hawaii Under Army Rule:* "For years the evil of prostitution was handled (sub rosa) by the local police who segregated the unfortunates in certain areas of the city. After the outbreak of war, a substantial number of prostitutes were brought to Honolulu from the mainland under military priorities. The Army decided that it was inhuman to confine prostitutes to a red-light district and hence lifted the ban.

"Private homes, some in the best residential districts of Honolulu were converted to houses of prostitution. There were so many rigorous objections from neighbors who were awakened nightly by visitors to the approved Army brothels that the Army decided "to return the 'jurisdiction' over this 'function' to the local police commission." When the police again segregated the prostitutes ". . . the city of Honolulu was treated to the spectacle of a three weeks' strike by prostitutes who picketed the police station and the office of the military governor with placards announcing their grievances." Nothing about any of these bordello capers ever appeared in the Honolulu newspapers.

Anthony reported that a February 8, 1943, proclamation partially restored civilian government. "General Delovin Carlton Emmons

*       *       *

endeavored to persuade the governor of Hawaii to take over the 'function' of regulating prostitution but the governor declined. As a result, the police were ordered to close the houses of prostitution, and substantial numbers returned to the mainland."

It is ironic that some forty years later, prostitutes, while no longer legal, continue to operate openly and are readily available to soldiers and sailors, who know exactly on which streets to find them in Wahiawa, on Hotel Street, and in Waikiki.

In Japan, during the years of reconstruction following World War II, the needs of men were not taken care of by houses of prostitution but by privately arranged liaisons. A retired Army colonel who had served in Japan during this period recalled: "Some of my contemporaries had various liaisons going, including some men who went with Red Cross girls and others with Japanese women. There were plenty of Japanese girlfriends among our officers, but we didn't see much of these couples socially. They seemed to be more private in these liaisons. Just before the first boatload of wives arrived there was quite a lot of cocktail buzzing about what the men were going to do about their liaisons. The so-called free love period was about to end. Most of the men I knew were able to make that jump back into their own lives after the war. A few, however, were not able to resume their marriages, and they ended in divorce. Then too there were wives who elected not to rejoin their husbands for many reasons, which included finding companionship with others during the time their husbands were absent.

"There were all sorts of liaisons, no question about that, but to paint the time as a hellhole of drunken orgies is just not possible—for it was just not true. For some reason the seasoned common soldier seemed not to be as aware of the temptations of the flesh as the younger troops might have been, maybe because they were more educated or because the jobs needed during the occupation tended to be of a more technical nature, with backgrounds required in sociology and law and order."

★                                    ★                                    ★

The colonel then added, "If you ask the military officially about any of this, whether it is Japan after the war or around any of the other bases today, the answer you'll get officially is nothing goes on. The military turns a blind eye. However, every fire base in Vietnam during the skirmish had its own village with women available. There is no way to know how much of what went on was by rape or by consent because rape was never mentioned."

In Japan, thirty years later, little had changed except more families were sent along with the men on the longer tours. There were plenty of husbands on year-long unaccompanied tours. In the 1970s, one Marine wife said she "crashed" Japan to be with her husband on an unaccompanied, one-year tour. Her passage over was not paid for. "We were expected to stay home in the states," explained Barbara, a vibrant honey blond. "I had a grand time working and traveling. Out of all of my experiences I'll never forget our tenth anniversary. We went out to dinner with four other very high-ranking military people and four very attractive women. I was the only woman without a corsage so of course I remarked about it out loud. I have this tendency to put my foot in my mouth. Silence. Dead silence. Not one of those officers was married to the woman he was with. They were 'dating' the military women and the nurses or the Department of Defense teachers. Having us wives there made it uncomfortable for them because if we were ever at the same base together—and the military was such a small world that often we would transfer together—we would remember seeing them with someone other than their wives."

## SIN CITY

Out of all of the bases that men talk about, the Philippines tops Japan in availability of sexual excesses. Of the many locations on the globe that are great liberty ports for the men, none rivals the sordidness of modern-day offerings in Olongapo—"Sin City"—in the Philippines. The Navy presence creates twenty-eight thousand jobs in

Olongapo and increases the revenues locally by an estimated $240 million a year.

Writing in the *Air Force Times* magazine supplement, "Life in the Times," Jay Finegan estimates there are fifteen thousand registered "hostesses," a euphemism for prostitutes, who are checked twice a month for venereal disease, and more than five hundred bars. The Air Force maintains the sprawling Clark Air Force Base with the city of Angeles providing the same entertainment as in Olongapo—and both right outside the gates.

"Walk straight out the front gate of Subic [Naval Base], in the Philippines, cross a bridge over a river that reeks of human waste, and there it is—Sin City, a mother lode of sex, sleaze, and cold beer for Seventh Fleet sailors," says Finegan. The bases "do their best to compete for the sailors' time. Subic, for example, provides the largest recreational complex in the entire Navy, and its many clubs feature inexpensive meals, slot machines, and floor shows that would do Las Vegas proud."

But the base recreational facilities cannot offer the bar girls "who are everywhere. A sailor has merely to walk into a nightclub and he has company for the evening, should he desire it. To a guy who's been floating around in the Indian Ocean for a month or two, this is the stuff of dreams. And it's cheap." One sailor noted the cost of a "complete weekend, with a girl, beer, the works" was forty dollars.

Reporter P. F. Kluge, writing in *Playboy*, quotes a club manager as saying: "We're trying to induce customers to buy pussy. The money's in pussy, not beer. So we started nightly boxing. . . . I've got fifty hostesses who are boxing. . . . I've got five girls who would rather fight than fuck. And—hey—if you want a good fuck, get a girl who's just fought."

In the same article, a Navy chaplain said, "Olongapo is a city of two hundred and fifty-five thousand people whose livelihood and economic survival are based on sex for sale. . . . Our conservative estimate is that there are sixteen thousand people involved in prosti-

★                    ★                    ★

tution . . . and the rest of the population in support services, renting apartments to girls and sailors. . . . The high tradition of the Navy, of officers and gentlemen, is being debased because of a lewd attitude, a failure to condemn wrong."

Ultimately it may not be the failure to condemn wrong as much as the specter of the rampages of AIDS that will slow down the business dealings in Olongapo—if anything will. The penicillan-resistant strains of venereal disease are a growing concern; AIDS has surfaced as a major problem from the Philippines. One colonel's wife, working as a Red Cross volunteer in a military clinic in Okinawa, reported that she had "screened a large number of young men around the age of eighteen who indicate they are in to check for V.D. Invariably they say they are just back from leave in the Philippines."

How much longer will it be before the AIDS virus decimates the troops who in spite of the apparent danger to themselves continue to frequent the women who are the primary sources of infection?

## WHEN WIVES TURN TO PROSTITUTION

While Olongapo may easily be one of the most depraved places on the globe, there are many other areas overseas that come in as close seconds. And, sadly, military wives have been drawn into the business of prostitution for the simplest of reasons—low pay, poverty, and a slim chance for legitimate work.

Overseas, the military wife (particularly wives of lower-ranked enlisted) is hit by double blows: the devaluation of the dollar has escalated the cost of living beyond her ability to afford the basics of food and housing, and United States government agreements with foreign governments restrict most employment *on base* to foreign nationals, effectively excluding the military wife from legitimate work.

While the devalued dollar caused suffering in all ranks, perhaps the hardest hit continue to be young wives of low-ranking enlisted. Assignment to Okinawa for Marines, as just one example, is an

**85**

unaccompanied tour, which means wives who join their husbands pay their own plane fares, are not eligible for on-base housing with fixed, affordable costs, and are not eligible for the cost-of-living adjustments paid to authorized service members.

There seems to be a callous outlook toward these unauthorized dependents of lower-ranking enlisted men. In an article, reporter Rick Maze quoted an unnamed Pentagon official who said that while the Army is aware that these non-command sponsored dependents are not being given full services "We don't want to do a better job. We want them out of there. We would rather they just leave than to demand services that we don't have the money or inclination to provide."

It seems that the nonauthorized dependents far outnumber those who are command sponsored. Only 3,000 of the 28,000 Army troops in Korea are on a two-year tour that enables families to accompany them. There are 9,500 command-sponsored dependents and 10,600 non-command-sponsored dependents the reporter said.

In September of 1985, the dollar could be exchanged for 242 yen; by May of 1986, the exchange rate was 168 and falling. A very substandard apartment that once cost six hundred dollars would be inflated to nine hundred dollars—without a raise in pay or household allowance to help defray the expense. That apartment, in fact, would take almost all of the young serviceman's pay, which, depending on grade and years in service, could be as little as $1,100 a month.

Even in the commissary, cost of food was exorbitant. As just one example, a half-dozen grapefruit cost thirty dollars. Fruit became a luxury. One author witnessed a woman and her three children shopping in the military commissary in Okinawa. The children were begging—not for a sugared cereal or candy or a special treat, which children are prone to do, but for an apple. Because of the excessive cost, the mother simply said, "It's too expensive." Listening to their pleas, she finally relented, picked up the apple, and said, "As soon as we get home, you can all share."

★                    ★                    ★

Why doesn't the military wife get a job?

She can't.

Legitimate work is seldom available to overseas military wives because Uncle Sam agreed to hire only foreign nationals on overseas bases. In addition, as David R. Schweisberg explains in the article "Weak Dollar Puts Women in Bar Jobs" in the May 27, 1986, issue of the Pacific *Stars and Stripes*, a newspaper for the military, "United States military regulations prevent service members from moonlighting, and dependent wives are barred from working by Japanese immigration law, and a United States ban on dependents working in any establishment serving liquor." In Japan, most available jobs on base, other than with the Department of Defense schools, were held by local Japanese women.

When parents have serious difficulties providing the necessities—much less the luxuries—what must a mother do to feed her children? If there are no savings, no legitimate jobs, some see the only alternative is to work in the bars.

Adjacent to military bases are clubs that cater to a clientele wanting sexual services and preferring Caucasian women. It was in these clubs that military women and wives of the servicemen allegedly worked as prostitutes. Overseas in Japan, Korea, and Okinawa, a bar girl is synonymous with being a prostitute. The article reported on the numbers of military wives and active-duty servicewomen "who have turned to hustling drinks as hostesses in exclusive nightclubs and sleazy bars" because the falling dollar is causing severe economic hardships.

Japanese investigators said the nature of the clubs' hostesses was such that many of the women doubled as prostitutes—a fact that military officials denied. Japanese sources said that "they believe some women use the bar work as a springboard for prostitution, earning up to three hundred dollars for a 'date' often arranged through bartenders." The bars mentioned are located just outside Kadena Air Force Base in the Nakanomachi "entertainment" district, which is said to

**87**

★        ★        ★

be "a crime-ridden red-light shopping and restaurant section." (*Parade* magazine stated that unverified sources indicate ". . . three hundred or more servicewomen, as well as wives of United States military personnel, have been working as bar hostesses to augment their income.")

It is obvious that the military was uncomfortable about the publicity generated concerning the adverse conditions in Okinawa that forced women to seek employment as bar girls and perhaps as prostitutes to bring home enough money to survive, for as a result of their forthright article, the editor of the publication and other staff members were relieved of their duties and transferred.

## MILITARY MARRIAGES: COMMUNICATE ONLY THE GOOD

In addition to all the stresses already mentioned that have an impact on military marriages, there is the additional problem of communication. Simply put, the military pressures wives not to communicate fully to their husbands but to withhold negative news while they are deployed. As just one example of the military controlling communication, the wife of an FBM (Fleet Ballistic Missile Submarines) submariner (who rotates three months at sea, three months at home) must send her familygrams, which are radio messages, the only communication possible while her husband is underwater on patrol, through the submarine's off-crew office. The wife fills out the familygram, which resembles a telegram. An officer on the off-crew is assigned to screen these familygrams. He may choose either not to send any negative news that might affect the husband's ability to perform effectively, or flag the message for the submarine captain, who may withhold bad news until the end of the patrol. The reason given to the wives is nothing less than national defense. The submarine patrols underwater in "enemy" waters, and surfacing to send the man home would reveal the boat's position. How can a wife argue against the defense of her country when all that is at stake is her health or the well-being of her children? (A standard joke among

&#42;                              &#42;                              &#42;

submarine wives is the totally negative familygram: FLAMES DE-
STROYED HOUSE, CONTENTS, KIDS CRITICAL, MY
SCARS HEALING, DOG SAVED, FIRE TRUCK WRECKED
CAR, ALL GOING WELL, FILING FOR DIVORCE, MISS
YOU, LOVE . . .)

Knowing of the Navy's proclivity for censorship, wives learn to
withhold negative information, a trait that eventually can errode
couple communication. Not all services restrict communication to the
degree the submarine service does. Most military men, even when on
remote assignments can receive phone calls from wives and if an
emergency exists, respond to it. The problem is one of immediacy if
the husband is thousands of miles away at a remote site.

## MARRIED STRANGERS

Most family counselors stress that one of the most important
aspects of a marriage is good communication skills between the
partners, and, as seen, the military erects barriers to good communications. Something else is at stake here. Because of the haste in which
many military couples marry, many military marriages may lack the
foundation necessary to forge good communication skills. Navy chaplain Dean Cook noted that it is difficult for normal dating to take
place because many nice young American women will not date
military men, knowing full well that often they will not be in town
long. Instead of time for an extended courtship, whirlwind courtships
and quick marriages to veritable strangers may be the norm.

Even if the man and woman have known each other for a lifetime,
growing up in the same town, having similar family backgrounds, the
military proclivity for frequent transfers makes it difficult for a couple
to grow together and strengthen a marriage. Priscilla Gates, marriage
and family counselor, explained why. "After extensive work with
military families, I realized that frequent moves and separations retard
the settling-in process that civilian couples encounter and solve early
in their togetherness. The military couple does not settle into this

**89**

shakedown [settling-in] phase until close to the time he is ready to retire. With the military couple so often apart, they have to establish ground rules late in the marriage without the euphoria of the newness of living together or the sexual excitement of the honeymoon period. As simplisitc as it seems, this lack of settling could turn the golden years into periods of unusual and unexpected amounts of stress and anger that they need to work through to keep the marriage intact. Sad to say, after all of the separation and turmoil of their early years, it is the twilight time of his military career when many military marriages flounder.

"When the husband is close to retirement, the wife is no longer needed as the primary care person; the children are usually high-school age or leaving for college; his job responsibilities are lessening; and she is left without a strong direction for her energies," explained Gates.

Also, a military couple with a history of years of separations encounter problems in raising children and in their sex life when they finally experience a long stretch of time together. For all those years he was gone, the husband was only a father figure, never a daddy at home. The wife was the primary care-giver. Now that he is home for good, he attempts to take over and "straighten out" the mess she made. Of course, she feels deep resentment and anger. Often during this chaotic time the children, who are barometers of their parents' feelings, are brought in for counseling because of problems they are experiencing at home or school.

In addition to problems with their children, overnight, it seems the couple's sex life has hit the skids. Sexual compatibility becomes an overwhelming problem.

"If someone is gone for more than fifty percent of the time, as many military men are, we can't say the couple has had a normal sex life," explained Gates. "It is a very real problem we find in the military. Absence certainly does lend an air of excitement to the sex

★                    ★                    ★

life. Who doesn't look forward to reunion with an air of romance after three months of being gone?"

With a husband's retirement, for the first time, the exciting honeymoon cycle is gone. The husband is home all the time, there are dirty dishes in the sink, a youngster is flunking, the dog has eaten a hole in the fence—reality has to be faced. The wife expects to be wined, dined, and romanced at the level she had been, a level that rarely continues in "normal" life. Because he was home so little during his long military career, she may never have told him that she didn't like making love in the morning, or that she was turned off by his smoker's breath. She withheld her negative comments because he was home such a short time.

He becomes totally involved in his work because the level of stimulation differs for him now that he is home all the time. This prolonged at-home time is when their different levels of needs show up. She may be horny all the time; he may be content with infrequent sex. Neither noticed their separate needs before because a high level of intensity was maintained in their short time together. If the couple does not have excellent communications skills, if the marriage was in trouble before this, then the marriage may flounder in the attempt to straddle these very divergent life-styles and needs.

"With military couples, I see the honeymoon pattern repeated over and over again. There isn't a leveling off to a 'normal' life," Priscilla Gates noted. "However, the woman is usually faithful to that marriage. But in the times between the honeymoon periods or during the times her husband is gone, she is not admitting her sexual needs. Sometimes the easiest way of restraining yourself is to deny the simple fact that feelings exist."

What is at risk here is not just the well-being and longevity of the marriage but the physical and emotional well-being of the military man and his wife. Women may be paying a high price for marriage to military men, for the following reports show that separations cause illness—not just emotional but physical as well.

**91**

★        ★        ★

## WARNING: SEPARATIONS MAY BE HAZARDOUS TO YOUR HEALTH

Several studies have separately arrived at the same startling conclusion: separations have a profound effect on the emotional and physical well-being of military wives.

In one study, Reverend Robert W. Bermudes, pastor for ten years of a church in Groton, Connecticut, home port for submarines, noticed that although separations were considered a normal way of life by members of the submarine community, the repetition of separations caused undue hardship and immeasurable damage to the family. His work as pastor brought him into contact with wives of men who served on one of three types of submarines: fast attack, diesel boats—both types operated at sea for seven to nine months of the year—and Fleet Ballistic Missile Submarines (FBM), deployed for three months at a time.

His study, reported in the *Journal of Pastoral Care*, noted that during the separation period the women regularly experienced excessive symptoms of anxiety that included "long periods of crying, tightness in the chest and throat, shortness of breath, and bowel problems." Other symptoms that surfaced included an increase in the number of headaches and backaches, occasional insomnia, periodic depression, tenseness, short temper, and weight changes.

As a result of his study, Reverend Bermudes developed a ministry to specifically help Navy wives during the separation period. Women's study groups were formed and a bonding was created among the women who met regularly. These resulting friendships helped women through the separation. As a result of an experience with caring people, the depression and loss felt were found to be less debilitating and severe. Unfortunately, only a relatively few wives benefited, for similar programs were not established at other bases.

In the *Psychiatric Quarterly*, Richard A. Isay, M.D., published *The Submariners' Wives Syndrome*, a landmark study in which he documented that more than half of the 432 women seen in the submarine

★                              ★                              ★

base outpatient clinic during the duration of his study were suffering from a reactive depression that manifested itself shortly before or after the return of their husbands from sea duty. The submarine wives showed up in the clinic with symptoms similar to those noted by Reverend Bermudes. In simple layman's terms, Dr. Isay says the wives' depression was caused by a guilty response to their unacceptable rage at being deserted and to their frustrated longings to be cared for adequately. But, said Dr. Isay, the submariner's wife cannot openly say or express her anger at being abandoned by her husband. It is not acceptable behavior. The wife is constantly being indoctrinated on the critical importance of her husband's work by other wives, lectures held by Navy commanders, as well as books and military wives' magazines. A "good Navy wife" cannot openly express her anger at being abandoned. One of the results of the unexpressed anger is depression.

"The fact that anger over deprivations is largely handled by repression and denial, and that any breakthrough of anger is a source of guilty preoccupation, is in part due to the Navy ethos that discourages a wife from verbalizing any feelings that might lower the morale or professional effectiveness of her husband," observed Dr. Isay. "The illness serves as a reproach to the husband, who on his return from patrol is witness to the effects of the previous months of deprivation and hardship. It is in a sense a silent, and therefore acceptable, protest."

Isay noted that sexual withdrawal and sexual inhibition when the husband returned from patrol were also used by the wife to protest his abandonment of her. Through their actions these women are silently saying to their husbands, "You deserted me, you bastard, and I'm going to get even."

In her doctoral dissertation of May 1979, "Separations and Reunions: Their Impact on the Submariner's Wife," Alice Ivey Snyder, Ph.D., anthropologist and submarine wife authority, looked at submarine wives in Honolulu, Hawaii, and documented a direct link between the amount of illness and medical problems experienced by the wives and the separation period. The women studied by Dr. Snyder were all said to be in good health at the time of the study. However, Dr. Snyder clearly documented the deterioration of the women's physical health during separations. When a couple was apart, the wife went to the medical clinic 5.4 more times than when her husband was home. This amounted to 17.21 illnesses and check-ups per woman for the year—almost fifteen of which were in the husband's absence. Wives recognized the link between separations and their emotional well-being, but *not*, says Dr. Snyder, the link to their physical well-being. Among the many problems she documented were rashes, ear infections, urinary tract and sinus infections, sprains, cuts, bruises, depression and sexual dysfunction when husbands returned.

"These many problems indicate in a physical sense how important the separation period is to the women. . . . Important life events, occurrences which are deemed important to the individual, such as separations and reunions, are stress producing," stated Dr. Snyder. "Their occurrence may predispose one to illness. If a life event is very important, or if several life events occur within a given year, it is probable that the individual will become ill. In that an FBM submariner's wife faces two separations and two reunions every year, in addition to other life events, it is possible that she may be predisposed to illnesses. She could be predisposed even more so during the periods of separation than [during] reunion periods for separation is regarded as more important, and therefore, more stress producing, than reunion. . . . One is led to the conclusion that the husband's being at sea is associated with a preponderance of illnesses."

Included in this litany of illnesses were back pains and other symptoms directly associated with sexual abstinence that followed a long period of regular sexual activity. "Cessation of active sexual participation by the woman can lead to a congestive condition of her blood vessels throughout her body, muscular irritation, muscular

*          *          *

contractions, and severe muscle spasms because of unreleased sexual tensions," noted Dr. Snyder. "It is plausible that many of a woman's physical difficulties in [the absence of her husband] are attributable to sexual tension, especially menstrual problems and backaches, which can translate to direct involvement of the primary sexual organs. It also appears plausible to expect these problems to be more severe immediately following departure of one's husband for sea when abrupt cessation of sexual intercourse is the norm and unresolved sexual tension may be highest.

"This situation is compounded by the woman's apparent unwillingness to utilize automanipulative techniques in [her husband's] absence or to admit to such tension and do something about it. Repeatedly, informant wives would comment upon their eagerness to resume sexual activity with their husbands but most of them denied any sexual needs existed when their husbands were gone or were unwilling to find some means of filling these needs."

The women in Dr. Snyder's study engaged in frenetic activities including housecleaning and sports to keep themselves in a constant state of exhaustion, which Dr. Synder interpreted as an "unconscious attempt to resolve that [sexual] tension."

It is interesting to note that Dr. Synder emphasized that "*no* [military] doctors [seen by the women] associated back problems with sea time of the men and that *no* doctors attributed *any* physical complaints to sexual continence and associated tensions. It appears that the doctors, too, fail to recognize that submariners' wives are fully dimensional individuals who have a sexual side even though their husbands are at sea."

## SEX AND THE "SINGLE" WIFE

There is perhaps no other life-style that promotes the possibility of promiscuity as much as the military. A lonely wife may go out simply for an evening of dancing and find her need "just to be held" leading her to a one-night stand. While temptations exist for both partners,

★                          ★                          ★

they may be less so for the woman kept busy caring for children. If she stays involved in the military community, she is more visible and may find it difficult to discreetly embark on an affair. Those factors, many wives said, mean that affairs are not as frequent among wives as one would think. Further, many said an affair often was an indication of a marriage in trouble.

The woman left at home alone runs head-on into the double standard of what social activities are acceptable for her, as opposed to those suitable for him. He can go bar hopping with the boys because it is an acceptable outlet. If she goes out for a drink while he's gone, she's labeled a WESTPAC (husband deployed in Western Pacific) widow and because of her loneliness is thought to be available for a one-night stand. Other wives say "Nonsense." They go out if they are comfortable socially in situations in which wives are encouraged to participate in couples' activities.

Mary, an Air Force officer's wife, said she would occasionally go out with a friend. "When my husband was gone for a year, I lived in a small college town in Iowa during the year I taught. I had an old friend—male—who would check up on me when he was passing through and take me out to dinner. Every time he came by, if we were out in the yard, my neighbor, who was a minister, would pointedly ask me in front of him: 'And what have you heard from your husband?' People do not really believe that a woman can have a platonic relationship," she added emphatically.

Living in military housing is even more of a fishbowl existence in a four-plex or eight-plex compound with neighbors who have time on their hands to watch the comings and goings of neighbors and gossip about them at coffee klatches. When Anne, wife of a senior chief in the Navy, was interviewed, she lived with her husband in a four-plex house on a large Navy base.

"Within the first week my husband got home from his last long deployment, my neighbor caught him as he was coming home to casually tell him: 'Your wife has been going out on you when you

\*          \*          \*

were gone.' Good old Fred played it to the hilt and really told off that neighbor. Of course she'd never believe that the man I was 'going out' with was Fred's school chum and best man at our wedding. Fred knew he'd be coming through and asked him to stop by and take me out to dinner.

"Now that you got me on the subject, I get really angry," said Anne as she paced her neat and pleasant living room. "We wives really get slandered. They call us WESTPAC widows and think we are easy pickups because we are so lonely. Let me tell you this," she said with clenched fists, "I don't know of one wife who has been fooling around. Most of the marriages are good ones that have survived over a number of years. It's damn hard being married to a Navy man. It's lonely. When I go out it's with a group of women. We have a lot of potlucks at other wives' homes. I do a lot with the kids. For a lark, a group of us saw male strippers. And we did go out for a couple of drinks at the chiefs' club. But the group I went out with went out together and came home together."

Sandra, an officer's wife who had to endure year-long separations from her pilot husband, laughingly called going out "getting rid of the poison in your system. You have to go out with the wives and have a really good time. You simply CANNOT sit at home all of the time."

Recognizing that they cannot stay home all the time, some wives find it comfortable going out at night with other wives. "I have known wives who hit the bars and see who they can pick up," noted Lila, the chief's wife. "They choose to play around as a way of life. Their husbands leave; the boyfriends move in. However, I see it as a matter of choices. You find something to do, you find friends with the same interests, go to the botanical gardens, go to the zoo. Some women can't stand to be without a man; some marriages last because the husband never finds out. It's not a majority of women who fool around—it's a small minority. When my husband was gone I went out dancing, but I never went out alone. I always went with two or

★                              ★                              ★

three girlfriends and we went as a group *and* we went home as a group."

Safety in numbers. If you succumbed to the stereotype, you'd hardly expect a man to find comfort in a group. But a new kind of Navy "wife," a man married to a female Navy chief (see Chapter 8), said going out in a group when his wife was gone saved him a lot of grief. "Going out with the other members of the Enlisted Spouses Club kept me out of trouble more times than I can tell you," explained Charles, a retired Navy chief who is the military "dependent" of another Navy chief. "We'd go out on Thursday night after bowling with the group. My wife was gone. I was with friends and they were determined to keep me out of trouble. They even chased the girls away from me. If I was out with the guys I could have gotten in trouble."

That feeling of having a group concerned about you was discussed by another Navy spouse. "Being a part of a sisterhood is the way I would describe it," noted Pamela. "Our group was really open in our conversation. At my first wardroom wives' coffee they gave each of us 'new' wives a present. We unwrapped the box and found a vibrator and instructions on twenty-two ways to masturbate! We just howled. The message was that it was safe to masturbate. Maybe we were an unusual group but we were able to say how horny we were. It sure beat playing tennis 'til we dropped!"

So many of the wives shared how difficult it was to maintain faithfulness to their husbands when they were separated. Many said they controlled their feelings by realizing an affair was too messy. Carole, an Air Force sergeant's wife, told of the desperation she faced after an extremely stressful period of time alone. "I was craving a hug. I needed to be held, needed a sexual release. One evening I found myself alone with a neighbor who was my girls' soccer coach. He's good looking, extremely sexy with muscular legs, a well-built chest, and a really great sense of humor. We started verbally teasing, but when it came right down to him making a move on me and going to

★                    ★                    ★

bed I just froze. It was weird. I couldn't be unfaithful to *me*. I thought not of my husband but of me cheating me. Instead, if you don't mind me talking honestly, I got a dirty book and masturbated. It was lonely, but it did help with the tension."

## STAYING FAITHFUL

Doing without love, without cuddling, without sex, without the home time is extremely difficult for the couple. With a strong sex drive, can a man or a woman be faithful while apart? It is a question frequently asked by the couples themselves who are often stressed to the limit. In talking to couples, they say it takes an honest relationship, true commitment to working together, and the knowledge that the marriage is a long-term one.

One submariner interviewed was in his late thirties and strikingly handsome in his khaki uniform. He served on an FBM submarine that kept him away from home half of the year for the three years he was on sea duty. In his single days, he said he had hit all the exotic ports of Europe, the Far East, Australia, and Bermuda.

"But the difference is marriage," he said. "When I was single, I did everything a bachelor can do. I sowed my wild oats before I married at twenty-six. By that time I was ready to settle down. And for the most part the married men I know on the boat are pretty faithful— they don't fool around. Those that do have marriages that aren't holding together.

"Separations are damn hard. You miss sex, love, and just plain being home. What helps are the long demanding hours and the pressure during the upkeep period of getting the submarine ready for sea. By the time you hit the rack you're too tired to think of sex. The time it hurts the most is when there is slack time, time to think. That's usually when we're off duty but since we're underwater there's nothing we can do about it!" he added with a boyish smile.

A thirty-three-year-old officer stationed aboard a destroyer often deployed six to eight months at a time said he spent "ten years as a

**99**

single sailor honkey-tonking around the world. When I met my wife I needed her emotionally as well as physically. When I leave her, she is constantly on my mind. We have a strong marriage and one that God plays a strong part in. I love the Navy, but I feel guilty knowing there is a large portion of our lives together that we are both missing out on. I know I should be home.

"The hardest time for me is during the watch on deck. I look into the sky and see her face. The only way I can buy the separations is that I'm doing it for my country. There are times when I'm physically hurting really bad but I have a sense of honor, a norm I've set for my own life that I will not be unfaithful. It would hurt her and I couldn't do that. Most of the married men I know are pretty straight—there's sort of a peer group pressure. The single guys are another story," he added with a wide grin.

## MILITARY AND MARRIAGES

Military and marriages—like oil and water. It was a single man's Army for so long; now there is a preponderance of women and children. Families. Uncle Sam is sometimes a marriage counselor, sometimes a sex therapist, but most often the bad guy who sends men to far-flung exotic ports that will only lead to trouble. The military couple is under a microscope as zillions of words are written on studies commissioned by Uncle Sam on military marriages.

So why do they stick with it? Being in the military is more than a job. For those who stay in and make a career out of the military, it is a patriotic commitment to Uncle Sam that ennobles the sacrifices made. Couple after couple interviewed mentioned the bottom line: love of country. They feel they were contributing during the time they served. Those who get out view patriotism as "pure crap" and not reason enough to put up with the military milieu. No two military couples interviewed were alike. Some survived the separations and developed stronger coping techniques; others erected an emotional wall that is never quite let down.

★               ★               ★

In order for the marriage to survive the couple must be willing to devote time and energy. Military marriages can work—if the couple makes the commitment to each other to survive the difficult times. But not all marriages are ideal. In some, tensions accelerate to the point at which the wife becomes abused in what can be termed a war on the home front.

"They'll never even know that I touched you. I can kill you and not leave a mark on you."

—SPECIAL FORCES SERGEANT TO HIS WIFE

H e didn't kill her this time.

For the moment she was safe, cocooned within a shelter for battered wives. Protected.

MaryBeth shivered. The bars on the windows splintering the moonlight looked strong enough to keep him out. The heavy wooden door had no handle on the outside—he couldn't get in. Like a litany, MaryBeth repeated what the shelter worker had told her: the shelter's address had never been given out, never given out. She could sleep undisturbed. MaryBeth eased back against the wall, carefully stretching her aching legs across the cot. Cradling a pillow across her chest, she fell asleep at last. When she slowly awoke it was to the sounds of her young two-year-old son and the murmur of women talking in the hall.

"How are you feeling? Ready for some coffee?" the concerned voice of the shelter director asked.

"Mmm," MaryBeth groaned. "Give me a minute." She slowly inched her legs to the floor and using her arms pushed her body into a sitting position. She gasped. Each breath seemed rimmed with fire, the bandages were so tight. When the tears started, she turned her face to the wall. No . . . more . . . tears, she vowed, willing them to stop.

"We got the prescription filled for you last night. It's there on the table. The doctor in the emergency room said not to be a martyr. It's okay to take a pill for the pain."

MaryBeth reached for the water, swallowed the pill, and eased herself up onto her feet. "Want to help Mommy, Peter?" she asked

★                                               ★                                                 ★

her young son. She took his hand and painstakingly inched her way down the hall to the bathroom. It was as bare as a men's latrine. Nothing fancy about the old red linoleum, the utilitarian sinks, the large square mirrors.

The mirrors.

God, was that her?

She looked at her misshapen face, the livid purple bruises, the line of fine stitches at the corner of her mouth. She unbuttoned her blouse. Her stomach cramped. Bile threatened to burn her throat. She held tight to the cold porcelain to stop the shaking.

"Mommy okay?" asked Peter, coming from the stall.

"Mommy *will* be okay," she answered in a voice calmer than she felt. That bastard.

She looked at the lank hair plastered to her skull, at the eyes that used to look out on a happy world. She hadn't laughed in a long time. She loved Larry dearly, but this couldn't go on anymore. There had to be a way.

Cautiously, she walked to the noisy day room that with the colorful toys and voices of the women seemed more like a nursery than a shelter. There were three other women with their children. The shelter could hold thirty. She helped herself to coffee and juice for Peter and looked around for a place to sit. With the animated voices as a background, her thoughts of last night's terror seemed out of place. Her screams had awakened the neighbors. The M.P.'s (military police) had arrived with blue lights strobing the tropical night. Larry drunkenly lashed out at them. Failing to calm him, they took him to the brig to sober him up. The military policemen took one look at the blood, her cut lip, and swollen eye and drove her to the emergency room. In the blinding lights of the E.R., the military doctor on call was gentle with his questions and his exam. He found the cracked rib, stitched her lip, and anointed the multiple bruises. MaryBeth remembered a nurse asking her if she would be safe at home. When

&#9733;      &#9733;      &#9733;

she said no, a call was placed to the shelter. A lady with the kindest eyes came for her and her son. For the moment, at least, she was safe.

Her safe house would be temporary, the shelter worker said. A few days' respite and she'd have to decide what to do. But at the very least this was a military community that had recognized the terror of abuse and had funded a shelter. She would get counseling and have time to decide. At least she had choices. At least she could reach out for help. At least she was not dead. Six military wives that same year were.

The wives who died were said to be abused, which is defined as assaultive behavior between adults in an intimate, sexual, theoretically peer and usually cohabitating relationship. Included are physical, sexual, psychological, and verbal as well as real or threatened destruction of property or pets.

Abuse has come out of the civilian as well as the military closet. Battering your wife is no longer viewed as a private affair on either a military base or in the civilian community. It is being reported; statistics are being kept. One book shocked the American public into a realization of how widespread and dangerous abuse is. That book was *Behind Closed Doors: Violence in the American Family*, co-authored by Murray A. Strauss, Richard J. Gelles, and Suzanne K. Steinmetz. The authors indicated that during the course of their marriages twenty-five percent of wives are severely beaten and that spouse abuse occurs in all strata of American society, from the college president to the blue-collar worker. Other books and studies since then say battering occurs more frequently. In her book *The Abusive Partner*, Maria Roy estimates that violence against wives will occur at least once in two-thirds of all marriages and that "one out of twenty-six women are beaten by their husbands or male companions each year."

Recent statistics state 5.7 million wives each year (including the military) are victims of some form of spouse abuse. Some 1.8 million women were severely assaulted. Add to that figure the women who are being abused but not reporting it and it is easily seen why spouse abuse is considered such an enormous problem.

The military has been ordered to keep statistics since 1982. Statistics count MaryBeth as one of the 14,382 military wives abused in 1986. But, say military personnel dealing with this war on the home front, statistics don't tell the complete story. For every one military wife with enough guts to report abuse as MaryBeth did, there are at least ten others—a possible whopping 140,000 estimated—who don't.

Why?

Military wives are scared.

If she keeps her mouth shut she'll have a roof over her head and food on the table. If she turns him in—or asks for help for herself—she jeopardizes his military career and their financial security. He could be drummed out of the military.

Working for the military is not like holding down a factory job. If a civilian batters his wife, the civilian police show up, intervene, take her to a shelter, and file a report. That's it. Unless he kills her and the story hits the paper, no one but perhaps the immediate neighbors know what happened behind those closed doors. A copy of the police report does not go to his boss at the factory. It does in the military.

Living in housing on a military base means no closed doors, no private fights. When MaryBeth's neighbors called the military police, they intervened in the domestic dispute, saw she was injured, and got her to the base hospital. The next morning after such a dispute the M.P.'s report will hit the commander's desk and, depending on how valuable the batterer is to the command, could be the basis of a court-martial offense or loss of a stripe for the man if he is a "loser" or a simple verbal reprimand if he is a "good troop." He could be declared unfit for duty or fined or simply ordered into counseling. His career could be over or his chances for promotion curtailed.

Lois A. West states in "Wife Abuse in the Armed Forces," a report for the Center for Women Policy Studies, "There is, perhaps, no other social institution in which an employer is as involved in the personal lives of his employees as in the military. The commanding officer is not only responsible for the job the service member does,

★                              ★                              ★

but also for his conduct and behavior. This creates a situation in which personal offenses that reflect on the military or on the work being performed go into a member's military record and affect his or her promotional chances." The fears of not being promoted, of getting a bad evaluation, of being drummed out of the service are all very real to the men who want to sustain a military career; these fears are equally shared by the wives.

If the abuser loses a stripe or a chance for promotion because a complaint was filed, the family income is greatly reduced. It may be years before he regains the stripe or is promoted. If the report of abuse affects the Officer's Efficiency Report (OER), it is the kiss of death. However, even today, many officers and enlisted men are permitted to stay until they complete their twenty years—especially if they are in a vital skills area. Without a chance for further promotion, at some officer ranks there could be a potential loss of salary of between three thousand dollars to ten thousand dollars per year. If the enlisted or officer does not regain his lost rank, his retirement income will also be reduced. Salary plus retirement security is a powerful inducement for wives to keep their mouths shut. Men soon realize that they can almost get away with murder, for many wives will endure abuse rather than lose their income.

As Sue McPherson, clinical services and outreach coordinator for the S.A.F.E. program (Services Assisting Family Environments) of the Parent and Child Center of Hawaii, noted in counseling abused military wives, "Time after time the spouse would say, 'Please don't tell his commander. It will affect his career. How will we pay the bills?' " If marriages break up, wives face the scary world alone with minimal income of their own. Explained in this light, it becomes very apparent why women cling to their abusers. If the military could find a way to punish the abuser and get him/her into effective counseling without financially punishing the family, more wives would seek help.

On the other side of the coin, wives have been known to threaten to report their abusive husbands as a means of coercion. As in the civilian world, the military must check carefully in case the abuse complaint is untrue. In 1989, at an Air Force base, a captain was accused of spouse abuse by his Filipino wife. When the matter was fully investigated, it was found that the wife had been threatening to file spouse abuse charges if her husband did not bring the rest of her family to the United States as his dependents. When he continued to refuse to do so, she brought the charge against him.

As serious as it can be for the man, the new awareness of wife battering is a godsend for the military wife. Even ten years ago the M.P.'s would have shown up at the door, talked briefly to the couple, and walked out, firmly believing that a domestic squabble was not any of their business. Laura Crites, director of a family violence program and a criminologist and sociologist who has worked exten-sively with abused military wives in Germany, noted, "Since the early 1980s, many M.P.'s have received sensitivity training in regard to spouse abuse." Initial training for enlisted Military Police is at Fort McClellan, Alabama. "At school, military police are drilled on the importance of working with other agencies in resolving individual cases of family violence. . . ." They are taught that the first priority is the safety of the victim, it was reported in MILITARY FAMILY. Their training procedure is based on the handbook "Crises Interven-tion," which is published by the International Association of Chiefs of Police. In the military as well as the civilian sector, spouse abuse is now treated with the seriousness it deserves.

## DOES THE MILITARY OUTSLUG THE CIVILIANS?

Is there more abuse per capita in the military? The answer, unfortunately, is yes.

An inspector general's report on domestic violence indicates that military service "is probably more conducive to violence at home than any other occupation." The study cites three major factors within the military that may lead to higher levels of violence: the authoritarian

★            ★            ★

setting of the military, the use of physical force as part of the military training, and stress caused by frequent moves of the military family. In addition, the report states "the high rate of alcohol abuse among military personnel makes the risk of spouse abuse high, to the extent that problem drinking and spouse abuse are found to be highly associated."

Wedged into the big picture of abusive life in America is the military male. The statistics indicate that apparently more military men abuse their wives than do civilian males. Why? A complete answer must consider all the contributing factors listed by the inspector general plus the most volatile component of all—age. More young men eighteen to thirty years of age abuse their wives; more young men eighteen to thirty years of age are concentrated in the armed services. With all the stressors combined, it is an explosion ready to be triggered.

Into this setting strides the young military male and his wife. While not totally in agreement with the authors as to the severity of the problem, from his vantage point of working with family violence, Ken Lee, M.S.W., director of the first Department of Defense funded, joint-services model program to combat family violence, sees family violence problems as young family problems. "All the studies pinpoint the salient fact that men thirty years old or younger are more prone to abuse spouses; 75 percent of the military is in this high-risk category as compared to only 25 percent in the national population. . . . There is this high concentration of military men in the at-risk ages. . . . You'd automatically expect a much greater rate of violence in military families than normal. Also, our numbers show up higher because we have a mandated reporting system that requires every professional to report abuse."

In addition to the age factor Lee believes that learned behavior has a great deal to do with violence. He points out that most of the abusers were themselves abused as children. "Much of the abuse can be seen as learned behavior, meaning kids that grow up in violent

**109**

*          *          *

households and witness abusive behavior as a way to solve problems frequently accept that as normal behavior."

One study zeroed in on military training and found that military personnel directly involved with combat readiness, as opposed to those who are in more professional or technical capacities, are more prone to wife abuse. Peter H. Neidig, Ph.D., reporting in his study "Domestic Violence in the Military, Part II: The Impact of High Levels of Work-Related Stress on Family Functioning," says: "In the area of family advocacy programming there is a growing awareness that within the military community, excessive work-related stress is often manifest in various forms of marital dysfunction including episodes of domestic violence. In our own work with Marine Corps Drill Instructors (D.I.) we have seen rather dramatic evidence of the effects of high levels of stress on the well-being of the family."

Dr. Neidig's study showed that the longer the Marine worked as a drill instructor the more abusive was his behavior toward his spouse and the less satisfying was the marriage. The longer he was a drill instructor the more he tended to treat her as he would a recruit. A drill instructor's job requires long, dedicated hours of whipping the young civilian recruit into a fighting Marine who will carry out each barked order without question.

Dr. Neidig points out just how demanding the role of the drill instructor is. "There are scripts that must be mastered and significant alterations in dress, bearing, voice, mode of interaction with others. . . . He is to demand perfection and immediate, unquestioning obedience. He is to be constantly alert to shortcomings among recruits and to point them out in no uncertain terms. He is to constantly [display] an almost superhuman level of dedication, endurance, and performance. The contrast between this role and the role of husband and father, which must be adopted in his personal life, is striking and the consequences of confusing the two, severe."

Does this training affect the wives? It most certainly does. Wives "detect negative changes in their husbands that they attribute to the

★                    ★                    ★

experience of becoming a D.I. They will often state with certainty that their husbands have become impatient, distant, demanding, and that they treat family members as they would recruits."

"The linear relationship between length of time on the drill field and increasing conflict and declining marital satisfaction suggests strongly that marital conflict and dissatisfaction can be accurately understood as occupational hazards for this billet," says Dr. Neidig. "And the rate of divorce among drill instructors—considerably higher than among nondrill instructors—"further attests to the uniquely disruptive influence of this duty on the family."

MaryBeth's husband was not a drill instructor but a sergeant in the Special Forces, an elite corps that rigorously trains men to fight and survive under the most brutal conditions.

Even after the men leave the military, their propensity to abuse carries over into their lives as civilians. Health-care professionals working in the civilian population find a correlation between abuse and military service. Bok-Lim C. Kim, M.S.W., in her study of spouse abuse of Asian-born wives entitled "Women in Shadows," found that ". . . men in the general population who abuse their partners often are or were in the military." It would help strengthen Kim's statement if there were more digging into the background of abusers by the people who gather statistics. But to date, that extra question "Are you now, or were you ever in the military" is not being asked of abusers. If it ever gets asked, most professionals say it will validate what is now only a strong feeling: that being in the military contributes to abuse.

It must be remembered that all of the military men who hold desk jobs were also trained in violence. And the violence spills over into the home. Laura Crites found a definite relationship between the nature of the military's work and the high rate of wife abuse. "The military accepts violence as part of its mission, has a higher tolerance for violence within its organization than the typical civilian organization, and I think this attitude probably carries over into family life."

**111**

★                              ★                              ★

Crites also named unique components to the military life-style that contribute to family violence:

1. Patriarchal values that reinforce the dominant male and the supportive and submissive/dependent wife.
2. Frequent moves over which the family has little or no control based on military needs and the military man's career.
3. Living in locations cut off from extended family support systems.
4. Extremely long working hours expected in male-oriented working environments with total commitment to the military organization and the toughness to withstand long hours, weekend duty, and little sleep being unwritten requirements for promotion.
5. Frequent separations due to remote tours and/or field assignments.
6. Overseas duty where wives are often isolated in a foreign culture with little or no support.
7. Inadequate income. Although the military has made significant progress in increasing wages and benefits, frequent moves, the difficulty wives have in finding work, and insufficient salaries create economic stress for many lower-ranking military members. It is not uncommon for an enlisted military man with a family to qualify for food stamps.

"The military also has ambivalent feelings regarding women that continue to dominate the military," says Crites. She says the military feels that women are the spoils of war, are less capable and need to be protected, and that the intrusion of women has emasculated the military. Official slogans still continue "unofficially" to state: "Join the Army and become a man," "The Marines are looking for a few good men," and "If the military had wanted you to have a wife, they would have issued you one."

The higher the man is in rank, the more serious the repercussions

★                              ★                              ★

of wife abuse will be on his career. So officer abuse tends to be handled quietly, away from official military records. Crites explains that older military men tend to have more resources and can seek civilian counselors. "We had a case in my area where it was one of the legal officers who was abusing his wife. He put her in the hospital a couple of times. That was never dealt with the way it is dealt with for the E-3s and E-4s. He was simply talked to privately. Overseas, abuse was a hidden problem, even though it was the most common problem the M.P.'s responded to."

In the civilian sector, researcher Murray A. Straus indicated that "wife beating is found in every class, at every income level." He documented that spouse abusers included the president of a midwestern university, a former prime minister of Japan, and the chief executive officer of a major company. What holds true for the civilian community should hold true for the military statistics. Almost all military abusers are enlisted men, rather than officers. One explanation is that statistics are kept on enlisted men. Officers have more to lose so abuse tends to be covered up by everyone concerned—the wife, the officers, and the military itself. For example, in January 1989, the authors were discussing the lack of statistics on officer spouse abuse with an Air Force colonel. "Oh, there are cases of officers abusing their spouses," he stated. "In fact, I know of two cases right now." Asked whether those two cases would show up in base statistics, he immediately became defensive, declaring, "Well, those officers have the right to not have this known; they have the right to their privacy." When he was asked if he didn't feel that enlisted abusers should also have "the right to their privacy," he immediately concluded the discussion by walking away.

"A number of difficulties appear when one tries to estimate the magnitude of the problems from the data collected by the Department of Defense," noted Beryce W. MacLennan, Ph.D., in his research report "Problems in Estimating the Nature and Extent of Family Violence in the Armed Forces." "For example, these data only relate

**113**

to reported cases. Since family violence carries a high degree of stigma and, if known, may jeopardize military careers, families and friends may attempt to hide any situations. At the command level, there are also mixed feelings about identifying cases. A large number of cases may indicate an effective program or a troubled command; a low number, a poor program or high morale. At the service level, chiefs of staff may not wish to give the impression that service life brutalizes individuals or places great stress on families, or that their service has more family violence than another."

In reported military statistics, the typical military abuser is predominantly E-4 or below in rank, under thirty, with minimal education, from any race, with a propensity for drug/alcohol abuse, an abusive family history, and existing at near-poverty level. Some 60 percent of the younger enlisted are eligible for federal food stamps during their first term of enlistment.

The typical abused enlisted wife is very young—often under twenty—with limited education. She is economically, emotionally, and socially dependent on her husband. Often, like MaryBeth, she married a virtual stranger, having dated only a few times. She sought marriage to escape prolonged, violent abuse by her father. She, like many other abused wives, was sexually molested as a child. There is no such profile on the officer's wife. But shelter personnel support the assumption that the officer's wife usually is better educated and is financially able to seek private counseling, so she doesn't jeopardize her husband's career by airing her dirty linen at a military spouse abuse shelter.

The first numbers on officers who abuse did not show up until January 1987 in the Department of Defense Spouse Abuse Statistics and there is no profile on the officer's wife. With all things considered, much of the abuse in the military never surfaces.

## THE MILITARY MOVES ON THE PROBLEM

The first military organization to show concern for treating spouse abuse was the Navy Department of Medicine, which began collecting

★ ★ ★

data in 1976 on suspected abuse cases treated in Navy clinics. However, there were major drawbacks. Reporting abuse was not yet mandatory. If Navy medical personnel did not directly question the cause of injury or if a woman did not say she was abused, reports were not filed. Also, it was noted that assigned health-care professionals were burdened with a heavy load of additional duties that lessened the attention they could give to spouse abuse cases, a tendency that unfortunately is still true today. No Navy-wide priority was given to the battered wife until 1979, when the Navy Family Advocacy Program was formed to deal with abuse—making it the first branch of the military that officially recognized spouse abuse.

In 1977, the Department of Defense Family Advocacy Committee was organized and took two years to draft a single policy statement on family violence for all the services. That policy (Directive, DOD 6400.1), signed in May 1981, mandated the organization of a DOD family advocacy program to address the problem of child and spouse abuse. Issued to all branches of the military, it ordered the creation of service-wide programs to identify, remedy, and prevent child abuse, child neglect, and spouse abuse. Because of this directive, most military bases now have some form of spouse abuse shelter and therapy program.

One of the most comprehensive programs was the one begun by the Military Family Resource Center, Office of the Assistant Secretary of Defense (Health Affairs), in August 1981, as a model program. It was based in Hawaii because the state was considered an ideal site for research: it included all branches of the service; Hawaii's isolation qualified it as a quasi-overseas assignment so programs would be tested that applied both to continental United States and overseas; and perhaps most importantly, military people were "trapped" in the sense that travel from Hawaii was more restricted than it would be from a stateside site with a flow of traffic on the interstate.

Ken Lee, as program director, began to implement the program through compiling a needs assessment. Two factors became quite evident, he explained. First was a need to establish a coordinated, coorperative approach for all branches of the service and to provide critically needed family advocacy outreach, sheltering, and prevention programs. The second need was to accumulate and analyze model program data in order to guide the development of other military family advocacy programs. Based on that needs assessment, six full-time, multidisciplinary teams were funded in 1981 to provide aggressive outreach services for family violence. Each team consisted of a social worker, nurse, and outreach worker all solely dedicated to dealing with family violence. As a second program component, monies were allotted to provide an emergency shelter for military wives, the one that sheltered MaryBeth. The third and final program component was a prenatal, secondary prevention program. Through routine prenatal screening activities, mothers-to-be, who were at risk for future abuse or neglect, were offered supportive services through a home visitor.

The comprehensiveness of these three program components is important because as other programs were established at bases around the world, budget restraints seriously watered down the effectiveness of single-focus programs. At some sites commanders chose to funnel money into drug/alcohol rehabilitation as more critical to the welfare of the troops. Some of the spouse abuse programs consisted only of a crisis hot line, others had shelters, still others had shelters and counseling. A crucial factor was how the ever-powerful base commander viewed the importance of intervening in spouse abuse.

The power of the base commander to make or break a program was emphasized by Laura Crites, who, from her experience of working with abused wives, found, "The majority of commanders I worked with in responding to individual cases were concerned and did want to take action to protect the wife. Their support became less apparent when counseling for the abuser was recommended, however. The military mission took precedence and few commanders are convinced that the mission is as negatively affected by spouse abuse as it is by

\*    \*    \*

drug and alcohol abuse." Other negative factors precluded a successful program. At some sites only volunteers were available to hold the spouse abuse programs together; at other sites the director wore many hats, resulting in a significantly weakened program.

One statement made by Crites needs to be amplified because it contains the kernel of what must limit programs for military families. "The military mission took precedence," she says. All of the military programs are based on that premise. It's butter or guns. The wife has become increasingly important *only* because her well-being has an impact on her husband's performance in the military.

Ken Lee explained further that "traditionally the military is not a human services organization. It is not in the business to provide social services to families. When the military can find a reason to justify providing services—such as mission readiness, increasing productivity of service members, and retention—then it becomes the military's business to run programs to help wives based on that intent. Only with the advent of voluntary military service did the military begin developing family service centers in the mid-1970s. Once the military did move on the problem it did in a comprehensive way and now, at least in the family advocacy arena, I think it is light years beyond what the civilian community is doing. The military defined the problem of abuse in a more global way as a family abuse problem mandating reporting of both child and spousal abuse."

If there is any criticism of military programs it is of the military's philosophy of treatment. Sue McPherson, who was with the agency in Hawaii when it was awarded the contract for clinical services and outreach in 1982, felt that the military program was only providing a Band-Aid approach to the problem. The premise on which the spouse abuse program was founded was that if the military member has a better home life, his job performance will be better. Said McPherson, "The military philosophy of treatment, and it is not ours in Child Protective Service, is you put a man in an anger management group for twelve weeks and give [the abused wife] a support group. Then

**117**

you put them together in a group for six weeks and they are all better."

They aren't "all better." Sue McPherson suggests that "cures" take much longer and because the military doesn't track the family to insure continuity of treatment, there is almost no follow-up of the couple at the new base. Often before even minimal counseling is completed the husband receives a set of orders to a new base. There is no established network between bases and no guarantee that a program of counseling will be available at the new base. More than likely he will continue his pattern of abuse.

MaryBeth got caught in this quandary. In an interview she said that the women at the shelter "were very warm and friendly and really tried to help. I chose to return to Larry because he said he'd go into counseling. I really do love him. Just at the point we were making great strides Larry got a set of orders. I really don't know what will happen. Because here he *had* to get counseling. Now what's going to happen to me?"

## PROFILE OF THE ABUSER

MaryBeth remains an enigma to the staff, for once she left the state, all contact was broken. She lives with a potentially dangerous, abusive man who has battered her more than once—the last time more seriously than the time before—and more than likely will again. Compounding the problem is the fact that Larry remains in the military with its authoritarian life-style rigidly controlling every aspect of his life. He, like other military men, feels he is not in control of his own life. He feels powerless because everyone who outranks him can and does give him orders. His life is controlled at each base. His insignia, uniform, short hair, and sticker on his car constantly remind him of his position in the military. Unlike a civilian employee, who is accountable to his boss only while on the job, each military member is under the strict control of, and accountable to, a superior twenty-four hours a day, including off-duty time.

★        ★        ★

What shows up repeatedly in spouse abuse cases is the need of the abuser to feel he is in control of some part of his life because he cannot find that control in the military; all that is left is his wife and family, but his wife also adds to his stress. As just one example: E-4 Smith lets off steam with a few beers with the guys. Money is tight; he really can't afford to buy a round. Still, he cashes his paycheck and treats his friends. After several drinks, he arrives home. His wife nags him for spending their money. As a social worker at Fort Carson, Colorado, explained, "His buddies add to his stress when he leaves early by saying that his wife has him 'pussy whipped.' He realizes that both his job and his family are causing him problems. His pay doesn't go far enough; his wife nags him about finances." Obviously, he can't control the military but he has power to control his wife—by fear of beating, sexual assault, or psychological abuse.

In the military milieu there is little room for the softer side of human nature. The rank structure of the armed forces "creates a greater awareness of power relationships in the workplace," notes Lois West. The colonel (or a chief petty officer) merely needs to bark an order and those below him in rank "snap to." If his commands are not met, the military has taught him that abusive language or actions will get results. At home he expects from his wife and family the same immediate response to his wishes. If his expectations are not met, he tends to become abusive. In interviews, wives of officers who were in command positions noted that their husbands' personalities had altered somewhat. As the men became accustomed to having their orders followed implicitly, to not being questioned, to having those lower in rank anticipating and ready to fulfill their every need at work, they expected the same treatment at home and many times became verbally abusive, barking orders at wives and children.

The officer is very aware of his position on the power continuum. Unlike the enlisted men who feel under the officer's thumb, the officer is responsible for every action of the men under his command—far beyond the kinds of responsibilities civilian supervisors ever encounter. Trying to explain the pressure, one lieutenant colonel stationed overseas stated, "I've got people I'm responsible for on my back every minute—the troops, their entire families. If they have a problem, it's my problem. If a man doesn't get promoted, he feels I let him down, even though I have no control over the promotion board. The wife of one of my airmen hung herself. I had done all the right things—counseling for the family, the chaplain, et cetera. The airman himself said things were going okay. Then she goes and hangs herself. My colonel calls and says, 'How could you let this happen?' How could I stop it? I'm only one man. Hell, I'm not in bed with them. And it's not always the big things. If someone's toilet doesn't work and civil engineering doesn't get it fixed quickly enough, the family involved sees it as my problem. It goes on day after day. Can't you see why when I go home at night, I don't want to see anyone? If my wife or kids even try to talk to me, I feel like knocking them across the room."

Add to this a strange twist of emotions expressed by the women. Wives interviewed said they felt they "deserved" to be abused if they didn't do their "job" as dependent wives as defined by the military. Enlisted wives especially feel they are second-class citizens, reports a 1982 survey of European-based military wives by the National Military Family Association. The military system continually reinforces that estimation. As military "dependents" their role is to support their husbands by caring for them and keeping the home "squared away." With few parenting or homemaking skills, these young wives "fail" miserably. When a Navy husband angrily slaps his wife because his "whites" are not white enough, or she can't keep the kids quiet when he is trying to sleep after standing the watch, she feels punishment is deserved. He was awake all night performing his patriotic duty; she has not fulfilled hers on the home front. She feels guilty for watching the soaps while he has been hard at work. Never mind that caring for an infant is a demanding job. She feels helpless and sees no way out. The cycle is vicious; she becomes more and more despondent, more and more depressed.

&#9733;    &#9733;    &#9733;

The military system doesn't recognize the woman except as an appendage to the man. Her only role as a military wife is to support him. At change of command ceremonies to honor the outgoing military commander, the "good" military wife is praised for being a well-dressed hostess, a busy volunteer, a dutiful and uncomplaining companion. She learns that conformity is rewarded by promotion.

Why doesn't she rebel? Why does she buy into the total control her husband exerts over her? She can leave—or can she? She cannot picture herself surviving on her own, for after years of abuse, she has no feeling of self-worth. She is truly a dependent—dependent on him and on the military system. As Helen McCallum, social worker and director of the shelter at which MaryBeth stayed said, "When I give talks, people just can't understand why women stay in these relationships. The audience needs to understand all the reasons why a person feels trapped."

Some officers' wives—in spite of their "higher" position within the military system—said they deserved their husbands' abuse. When a Navy commander screamed at his wife, "I didn't get promoted to captain because of your inability to entertain and handle your social duties as well as other wives," she meekly accepted the guilt. She too felt she had somehow failed.

## A TRUCE

Raising the consciousness of the military on the matter of women/wives is going to take time. Being able to even adequately care for the battered and establish prevention programs will take even longer. Every major military base has some form of program to assist the abused military wife. If there is any criticism it has to include the immutable fact: money. Budgets are stretched thin and may get thinner. As was pointed out, the military is not in the business to provide human services programs. It is in the business to produce fighting machines. Money must be spent for military readiness before it is spent on families.

★         ★         ★

Because of the lack of money and qualified people at many bases, some programs are limited to a Band-Aid approach. The military currently funds only short-term support for the wife and counseling for the abuser. Lack of follow-up funds and adequate personnel make it impossible at this time for any long-term therapy. An abuser is required to attend anger management classes only long enough to look good on paper, with minimal follow-up and no tracking of families from base to base.

Some sites are hampered by having only volunteers; when their husbands are transferred, the programs waver until other equally committed volunteers can be found. At other bases, directors of programs for abused wives also handle other family-related programs. Having to wear many hats greatly waters down their effectiveness. But when programs work they work because good, caring people help alleviate the suffering of the abused military wife.

On the plus side, in addition to the pilot program begun in Hawaii in 1981, there are many fine programs run by caring people. At the national level, funding was provided in 1983 to establish the Military Family Resource Center in Washington, D.C., with a three-year demonstration grant by the National Center on Child Abuse and Neglect and the Armed Services Department of the National Board of the Young Men's Christian Association. This clearinghouse of help and information continues to operate today, disseminating information as to where wives can go for help as well as information on the latest research projects to aid professionals.

"A program that works," is the way Commander E. A. Olander, Navy Chaplain, describes AMENDS (Abusive Men Exploring New Directions) at Camp Lejuene, North Carolina. The program was but one of several directed at helping the family. The AMENDS program was based on three areas, behavior regulation, behavior modification and then finally, behavior goals clarification.

Is there an answer? Not an easy one. There is a lot that has to be done on both sides of the fence. Funding needs to continue, profes-

\*                                        \*                                        \*

sionals need to keep researching the problem and solutions, programs have to stay in existence. They are helping. But just as important, military wives have to speak out. If nine out of ten wives continue as in the past to silently endure abuse, the military will fund other more "necessary" programs.

Military wives sacrifice a lot to keep families in the service. In return they are entitled to physical, sexual, and psychological security as women—not just as dependents whose sole job is to keep the military man functioning as a cog in the machine of war.

★                                    ★                                    ★

". . . Whither thou goest, I will go; and where thou lodgest, I will lodge; thy people *shall be* my people, and thy God, my God."

—THE BOOK OF RUTH, 1:16

E melia perched on the straight-back chair, feet barely touching the floor. She sat with her back rigidly straight, hands folded primly in her lap as the nuns from her private school in the Philippines had taught proper young ladies to do. At the beginning of the interview, she seemed as young and as vulnerable as a typical American teenager. As the hour wore on, she struggled as a mature woman of thirty-two with the emotional upheavals of marriage to a Navy lieutenant. She was reluctant to be interviewed because she was not used to talking about her private life. Finally she agreed, if her name would not be revealed.

Briefly, her eyes made contact, then she looked at her hands. "After two years of being on the same submarine, they still do not know me. Some wives are nice and make what you say—small talk. Other wives ignore me," she whispered. "I cannot take this American indifference for me. My parents are schoolteachers. We live in Manila in a fine home. I am a graduate of a fine college. But because I am a Filipina, the American wives consider me as nothing more than a bar girl because so many of the women the G.I. married came from Olongapo. They will not say this to me. To my face. They whisper and I hear. It is not right."

Emelia smoothed the linen skirt and painstakingly chose each phrase as if one wrong word would shatter the picture she was struggling to construct. "I think . . . no, I know, we have love in our marriage. My husband is a fine man. My parents were not happy at first, but now it is okay. I did not know—what is the word meaning more than lonely? Desolate, that's it—how desolate it would be,

**125**

alone, away from family. I left everything. I came from such a big family. We were always together for such happy times. Here we don't know anyone. It is so lonely, *especial* when he is gone. It is okay now but when my husband first left on patrol, I was desolate."

Emelia said she has more material goods in America, yet as she phrased it, "My heart is hurting." Even the church is not as comforting as she remembers from home because it is so different, but she is gradually finding a small group of American women who have befriended her. There are many problems to work through, but the sense Emelia imparted was that she and her husband will make it as a couple.

What Emelia and her husband Tom have is a sound relationship that had time to build. Tom met Emelia at the university where she was completing her studies and dated her for almost two years before they married. They also took the marriage course offered at the Subic Bay Naval Base. Another plus in their favor was Emelia had a solid command of the English language, which many of the foreign-born wives do not have. From all indications, Emelia and Tom have built a solid foundation for marriage, which is not always the case with so many others.

Being a foreign-born wife of an American is difficult. As long as the husband is stationed in her homeland, a wife has the support and comfort of her family and friends. It is when the man is transferred to the States, or to an assignment in a land foreign to her, that her difficulties compound. Even with all of the difficulties, the European wife's adaptation to American ways is usually not as traumatic as that of her Asian counterpart. The culture of the United States is, after all, rooted in Europe. (An article in *Soldiers* magazine indicates that marriages requiring the least adjustment are German-American, because the couples share much the same culture.) Probably the biggest plus for the European-born wife in her introduction to American society is the fact that she looks "just like us."

Because of the color of their skin, many of the European wives

     *                          *                                     *

interviewed said they could blend into a crowd until their accented English gave them away. However, they persevered, fine-tuned their English and their knowledge of the customs of their new land, and blended into the culture. As one German-born wife, married in the late 1940s, bluntly stated, "At least my mother-in-law knew the children had a good chance of being blond and blue-eyed. That made me more acceptable to his relatives, even if I was German, than if I had been from Japan. When at social gatherings if I didn't have to say much in English, people thought I was just another American. Even with my accent, several people thought I might have been from Minnesota or Michigan."

As she mentioned, language can be a major barrier for the European bride until she masters her new language. A German-born wife of an Army warrant officer said, "I knew some of the simple words or phrases when I came to America in 1956. I could say 'hello,' 'please,' 'thank you,' ask for the bathroom, and a few other things. Going shopping or out to a party was a real trial for the first year, but I went to night classes at a local high school in Massachusetts and soon was able to hold my own in a conversation. Now I'm very comfortable in English."

For those brides who speak English fluently—and many do—the adjustment is much easier. For British, Australian, or New Zealand-born brides, language is hardly a problem. As an English-born wife of a retired sergeant said, "Although your accents were quite atrocious, naturally I understood American when I came over in 1948."

Nanette, a French woman, had no trouble with English because she was a translator for the American Army in France and could speak English well when she met and married her husband in 1954. She did not encounter prejudice when she announced her wedding plans, but she did have to deal with profound grief from her parents, who feared they would not see her again, as well as wade through the bureaucratic laws of the Catholic Church. Even with her knowledge of the English

**127**

★　　　　　　　　★　　　　　　　　★

language, she still had some surprises in store for her in learning about American customs.

Although most foreign women had prepared for the move to America and learned the language and customs, once they moved to the States, they suffered from homesickness. "I missed England so much," one wife said. "Just to see my parents and walk down the same streets for one day was all I wanted." Several wives from Germany and France had been "just devastated" and "unbelieving" when they found themselves a continent away from their lush green countrysides and settled with their husbands in arid military stations in the American Southwest. "It was so lifeless, so unnatural," one German-born wife explained. "I couldn't believe it was so brown; I was used to pine trees all around."

This homesickness was alleviated if the husband was again sent on a European tour or if the bride's family could occasionally come for a visit. "There were some real bargains on plane fares to Europe in the 1970s, so my parents have been over for several visits, and the children and I have gone home on two occasions to see them," said the English-born wife of a Air Force major. The German-born wife of an Army master sergeant said, "We've had three tours in Germany, so I feel like I actually live in both cultures. I've not suffered too much from homesickness because of this."

Some ten or twenty years ago, the military did not have as many special programs as it does now for the foreign bride. Each adjustment to a new environment is obviously up to the individual but after interviewing scores of women, it would seem that European brides, on the whole, have an easier time adjusting to life in America than do Asian ones.

## THE EXODUS BEGINS FROM ASIA, THE PACIFIC

The marriages to foreign-born wives began as a trickle in the late 1800s when the American military first began to mobilize troops overseas. Long, lonely stretches of time in the Philippines, China,

Hawaii, and Europe were assuaged by legitimate as well as "jawbone" marriages. These numbers increased as large concentrations of occupation troops in Japan after World War II plus those involved in the Korean and Vietnam conflicts added Asian-born wives.

The numbers of these marriages continue to escalate. Nearly a quarter of a million Asian and Pacific Island women have become brides of American servicemen since World War II. (The terms "Asian wives" or "European wives" are misleading, for these wives are not "Asian" but Japanese, Korean, Vietnamese, Thai, and so on, just as "European wives" are French or English or German.) The largest number of wives has been of Japanese origin, with those from the Philippines running a close second. Wives from Korea, Vietnam, and Thailand total between eighty thousand and ninety thousand since 1950, although the figures for Vietnam and Thailand mainly began around 1965 with the rise in American activity in Vietnam. Two hundred brides a month "matriculated" through the required marriage course from just one base in the Philippines. Another estimate is 1,000 marriages are performed annually at Subic Bay. An average of three hundred and fifty marriages per month took place on the Korean peninsula in 1987; on Okinawa the estimate was sixty per month. Pacific Air Forces (PACAF), in a study published in 1982, estimates that one-fourth of the command's marriages overall are bicultural and on some bases overseas this figure could rise to one-half or higher as the men tend to homestead close to their wives' homes. The mountains of paperwork that once stonewalled marriages overseas have been reduced to just an annoying formality.

Why do they marry? He gets a submissive woman. She gets money, a base I.D. card, and a way to get to the United States—reasons not so different from those motivating other foreign-born women from economically depressed countries.

Parents often ask why their sons couldn't marry nice American girls. Weren't American girls good enough? Part of the answer is simple: few available American women overseas, with local women

**129**

being the only accessible dates and mates. One trooper found the woman of his dreams, a pleasant person whose smiles made up for the language she did not understand. So he married. Unlike American culture, where the man is often head of the family but the woman is head of the household, Eastern culture tends to emphasize the male role, with the man as patriarch, leading the household *AND* the family. According to an article in *Soldiers* magazine, this may be the main reason some soldiers marry Oriental women— "because they like power and control."

Additionally, low self-esteem may be a reason the enlisted marry foreign women. Consistently outranked, following orders but never giving any, they find little in the military structure to boost self-esteem. Men who have little or no opportunity to show leadership in the military suddenly are expected and encouraged to be boss at home. They find their "little China dolls" very submissive women who put them first—something they won't find in many American women.

How well do these marriages fare?

Not very well. When the woman is moved from home, it is extremely difficult for these marriages to survive. One study conducted by the Asian-American Mental Health Task Force in Washington State said that half of the married Asian women who responded to their survey were not happy with their marriages. Captain Daniel B. Lee, A.C.S.W., further stated, "It is generally understood that most of these marriages [to foreign-born spouses] fail to succeed and only a few of them are reached for adequate services." Problems compound. Unlike American military wives who journey to foreign lands, setting up an American oasis, the foreign-born wife has little to sustain her. Lodging among her husband's people is a traumatic experience. Some brides have made successful adjustments to their new environments, but others struggle as marginal women—caught between two cultures, no longer fully part of either one.

If a couple continues to live in the wife's homeland, the marriage is

★                    ★                    ★

far less traumatized, for she is surrounded by family and friends. Great numbers of American servicemen buck the system of moving every three years and "homestead" overseas by finagling repeat orders for the same base. Because the military recognizes relatives as dependents, base facilities overseas are burdened with caring for vast numbers of extended families. The American taxpayer is picking up the cost of free medical care and free housing for these new dependents. And often the husband's pay must stretch to feed his wife's relatives.

As if money was not a serious enough issue, add the chasm of communication between two different cultures. First of all, they both harbor preconceived notions of each other. The American G.I. marries what he calls his "little brown-skinned baby" because she is untouched by the liberated American female; she pictures a man who will deliver her from poverty, pay the bills, and keep her *and her family* fed. The wife pictures a very extravagant life-style when she hears her husband talk about America. He tells her his family has two cars. She envisions Cadillacs; reality is a ten-year-old Ford pickup and a Toyota hatchback. She has seen lavish homes in American-made movies; the reality is she must live in cramped base housing. He knows his family will love her; they despise her. He was very pleased with her dependency on him overseas; now she is too dependent or struggles to become more independent, angering her husband. As the husbands lose control of their "China dolls" they often become abusive.

Bok-Lim C. Kim discussed perceptions in "Women in Shadows," a handbook produced for the National Committee Concerned with Asian Wives of U.S. Servicemen. "The majority . . . marry [Asian and Pacific Island women] as a way of escaping from what they construe to be 'bossy, domineering, and castrating' American women." Kim admits some small percentage marry wives out of love and "a positive and idealized image of the Oriental woman and her culture"; however, she condemns most of the men for wishing to be "catered to without reciprocating" and harboring both "conscious and

**131**

unconscious disrespect and prejudice against their wives' cultures and countries." When Asian wives were asked to comment on these statements by Kim, many interviewed agreed with her analysis.

Breaking through these stereotypes is tough because rarely has either party the full range of words to communicate. Often the American male is satisfied when his new bride learns the basics of English so he doesn't have to learn her language. In order to shop or talk to a doctor, most wives quickly master rudimentary English. What literally gets lost in the translation are the depths of emotions and cultural differences. For many Asian-born wives isolated from contacts with their families and friends, communicating in English is only a veneer, revealing little emotion. There are so many nuances to language that many foreign wives cannot fully communicate their feelings to their husbands, who are supposedly closest to them. Unable to fully express her feelings in English and isolated from familiar customs and contacts, the Asian-born bride lives a lonely existence in her new land. Unlike an American bride, who might more readily tell her troubles to a friend or a neighbor, it is a custom of the Asian woman to keep problems to herself. So it is very unlikely that she will take the initiative of joining any outreach programs being offered by the military.

Traditional ways of viewing the world or of expressing emotion in the East and West are difficult to comprehend on both sides. Perhaps this can best be illustrated by the example of one Japanese woman who as a new bride was forced to spend many months in a small midwestern town with her American mother-in-law while her Marine husband was at sea. It was a very difficult time for both of them, but while his mother complained copiously about her new daughter-in-law, not one word of complaint came from the bride. When questioned about her mother-in-law's petty comments, she always gently replied, "Mama-san good to me. I not have problems."

Japanese-born military wives could see nothing odd about this, explaining that it involved a problem in communicating cultural

★                    ★                    ★

differences. "Japanese feel that it does one good to suffer sometimes," explained Sumiko, wife of an Air Force senior master sergeant and organizer of classes to help Asian-born spouses. "You Americans do not want ever to suffer, so you would complain and try to change things. We feel suffering comes to all; it strengthens a person to suffer. So naturally the bride would not have complained about her mother-in-law but would have suffered in silence. Then too, Japanese not show emotions as quickly as Americans. The wife would not have told anyone if she had been hurt by what the mother-in-law said or did."

Although easily able to make themselves understood, almost all Asian wives interviewed apologized for not being able to speak better English. All problems, even the smallest ones, become intensified when a wife understands and speaks only a little English. Social gatherings are particularly stressful, and wives recounted numerous incidents where they had used the "wrong" American words and felt embarrassed. Many also stated that some Americans apparently felt uneasy because they were unable to understand the Asian wives' attempts at English and avoided getting in conversations.

Lisa, a Filipino wife who is employed as a counselor and speaks English fluently, explained that she constantly finds herself at parties with an American military wife who, when Lisa says anything, will deliberately turn away from her and ask those standing nearby, "What did she say?" Of these awkward moments, Lisa said, "I think she deliberately tries not to understand me. Everyone else seems to have no problems. I avoid her if possible. When I can't, I merely smile, say 'hello,' and then move away."

All of these problems isolate the Oriental wife. She may withdraw from society after a few attempts to communicate fail. Army Major Dwayne D. Marrott directed a needs assessment of foreign-born wives, when he served as division psychologist at Schofield Barracks, Hawaii. His survey noted a "basic lack of awareness of military services available . . . and only nineteen percent of the Korean

★                              ★                              ★

respondents felt they had a working capability with the English language. A sense of dependence, isolation, and alienation is thus suggested for this group."

If these women are unaware of available help, live off base, or perhaps have to travel without their husbands, it can be a truly frightening experience. "I remember when we were stationed in Oklahoma, and my husband was sent TDY for a while," one Okinawa-born wife reminisced, recounting her feelings of isolation. "We not get on base because his rank was low at that time, so we were in civilian community away from anyone who might have helped on base. It was really scary for me. I couldn't sleep at night, so I stay up all night and sleep daytimes. I run out of money and can't write name of bank so I get more. I not drive. I know no one around me. I know everyone say, 'Don't worry,' but I do. I lose weight, was down to ninety pounds. I feel so alone."

A Vietnamese wife related a time when "I remember my husband and I had very bad fight. I had no close friends where we were stationed. Naturally, I couldn't call my mother or family in Vietnam. I finally called cab and went to Holiday Inn. I felt so alone." Those words—"I felt so alone"—would be spoken again and again by Asian-born wives.

For some the feelings of isolation become so intense that attempted suicide or suicide is the result. One thirty-eight-year-old Korean wife of an Army staff sergeant stationed in Florida found she was unable to make friends with people of her background or her husband's background. She felt what the psychiatrist treating her described as "a sense of inadequacy, social deprivation, and loss of self-control." When she learned of the serious illness of her blind father back home, she attempted suicide. Upon recovery, she revealed her feelings of guilt for leaving her impoverished family behind while thinking only of her own happiness. Since she could not return to Korea in her body, she tried to at least free her soul to return.

A thirty-five-year-old Korean woman in Honolulu, married to an

*          *          *

enlisted man, succeeded with a horrible death. In the cool, predawn darkness of a Honolulu morning, she seated herself on the edge of the backyard picnic table. With calculated, choreographed movements, she drenched her body and clothes with kerosene. She struck a match. Within moments flames engulfed her. Searing pain wrenched agonizing screams from her smoke-clogged throat. By the time the ambulance arrived she was dying, burnt beyond recognition, unable to be saved. She lingered for a day, then died.

Obviously not all foreign-born wives are suicidal nor do all suffer from severe depression. But their overwhelming sense of obligation to family makes them feel guilty. They try to provide for their families. The American G.I. quickly discovers he's married her *and* her family, which can adversely affect the marriage. Navy Chaplain Merle Metcalf explained: "The Filipino has a great sense of family, much more than the American. Although married to an American military man, the Filipino-born wife will do whatever is necessary to help out her family. Let's say her Navy husband comes back from sea duty and wants to buy a new car. He has sent money home to her regularly to save for a down payment, and now is the time to buy. She comes up with several reasons why this is not a good time, but he insists. Finally she has to tell him that she has given her family a good portion of the money he has sent her to be saved. Someone in her family was ill, she had a request from a cousin for money to help send his son to college, a hundred different problems could have occurred. This may be difficult for her husband to accept. We Americans teach independence from family; the Filipinos are taught that each family member should help care for the family."

When questioned about their allegiance to family, almost 90 percent of the Filipino-born wives interviewed indicated that they agreed with Chaplain Metcalf and stated that they felt a strong sense of commitment to their families in the Philippines.

Asked if he could recommend a solution for this cultural problem, Chaplain Metcalf said he ususally counsels couples to try and set up a

**136**

specific amount of money that the wife can feel is her own—to send to her family if she so wishes. If the cultural differences of Filipino family allegiance versus American family independence cannot be resolved, the marriage may have little chance of surviving.

## PREJUDICE ON ALL FRONTS

While many of the young women ask for their parents' blessing, not all receive it, which adds an additional stress to the marriage. As with American families, many Oriental families are offended and hurt by their daughters' selection of foreign mates. (Interviews indicated this was particularly true of Japanese and Korean families; to a much lesser degree with Filipino families.)

"My father was so upset," related one Japanese-born wife of an Air Force tech sergeant. Having met her future husband through classes they were both attending at a university in Tokyo, she got her professor to intercede for the couple. "After that my father feel better about marriage but still we only have small reception." Another Japanese wife whose father was dead told of her family not giving consent, even after the military man had formally met all of them and asked permission to marry her. "We started papers secretly, but I know I have to be twenty before I can marry. Finally my mother gave consent and we finish paperwork to marry."

The Korean wife of a marine lieutenant confided that her father has never really forgiven her for marrying a foreigner. Married now for five years and with a three-year-old daughter, she was planning a solo trip to visit her parents. "I have to get there shortly as I am nearly three months' pregnant," she explained. "My father says I can come home to visit only if my pregnancy is not showing. He wants to keep up the appearance that I have not married an American and if I were very pregnant, he could not do that."

Chu, wife of an Army lieutenant colonel, had a similar experience. "Although he didn't say much, I could tell my father was not pleased about my upcoming marriage to an American. Speaking fluent En-

★                              ★                              ★

glish, Chu continued, "He knew I was twenty-six and my boyfriend was twenty-nine, so he finally said that we should be old enough to make up our own minds. All of my family felt that I would leave and never see them again." (Chu has never been able to return to Vietnam, and her father died in 1981 without seeing her again.)

Perhaps the hardest problem for the Asian-born wife in a Caucasian culture is her Oriental appearance. Certainly she stands out in a crowd and many times becomes a curiosity for Americans not living near an Oriental population. While possibly well meant, the questions asked about her country by countless numbers of people she meets only serve to make her feel even more a stranger in what is to be her new home. For the Japanese bride, some forty years later, American memories of World War II affect how she is accepted (or not not accepted) by some Americans, even the military. As one American-born military wife said, "I was old enough to remember the newsreels of the bombing of Pearl Harbor, and I find it hard to think of those people as friends." Several others who, with their husbands, had been stationed in Japan made comments such as: "I can't believe they truly like us; you know they must be angry about Hiroshima," or "After all, we won the war, and we are now still in their country in large numbers. How would we feel if we had thousands of Japanese troops stationed in, say, California or on the East Coast?" Naturally these comments are not made in the presence of Japanese wives nor is there usually any overt show of prejudice or discrimination, particularly by those in uniform.

Still, many Asian-born spouses feel there is only a thin veneer covering the deep-seated prejudice of the white American toward the Asian. The husband of one Japanese wife tried to explain: "The exclusion is subtle so that at times you may think it exists only in your mind. It's hard to see. It's sort of withdrawal—a moving away from us by both the wives and the husbands."

Does this prejudice or "subtle exclusion" have an impact on the husbands' chances of upward mobility in the military? One Army

**137**

colonel bluntly stated: "As recently as ten years ago, it might have, particularly in the case of officers. It doesn't matter for the enlisted men, or not as much. Today, it actually might be a help. One had better be very careful not to show any prejudice against a fellow officer married to an Oriental."

A Navy captain said, "In the 1950s or 1960s, marriage to an Oriental could have killed most officers' careers. Now there are a few men who have reached high ranks who are married to Oriental women. Of course, everyone knows of General Claire Chennault and the Flying Tigers. His wife was Chinese. I believe there are still those exceptions."

"A lot of enlisted men are married to Asians, but it's difficult if an officer marries an Oriental wife," a Marine Corps colonel commented. "Most people assume all Asian wives are B-girls; many are not. Many times the social class of the wife is above that of the husband. I don't think the husband's career is necessarily hurt by the marriage, not today. But the prejudice is there—maybe not so you can see it—but it's there!"

Sometimes the prejudice is so blatant that it is like running into a brick wall. One Japanese-born enlisted wife told of attending a party that was being hosted by her husband's commander. "I not want to go, but he insist. This was soon after we marry, and I know I not speak English very well. When he introduce me to his commander's wife, I speak to her but she not say a word to me. She just stand with her arms folded across her chest and look at me. When I go home, I cry. My husband tell me she is always like that, but I not go to any more parties for long time." Whether this particular commander's wife was prejudiced and intentionally rude, or whether she was merely inept in this social situation, the result was the same. The Japanese wife felt the impact of hate and indifference.

A Filipino wife told of the terrible hurt she felt when meeting her American mother-in-law for the first time. The woman blurted, "How could my son have married an Oriental?" Asked if the relationship

★　　　　　　　　★　　　　　　　　★

between the two women had improved over several years of marriage, the wife thought for a minute and then, shrugging, said, "No. I try, but nothing better. I still Oriental."

Chioko indicated that she had met almost no overt prejudice but could "feel something there." While her husband told her several times that she was just imagining prejudice, she felt it showed in "the way the other American-born wives ignored me, ignore what I say. I know I am small [in size], but they act as if they can't see me."

This feeling of prejudice is verified by at least one study. Major Marrott, in the survey referred to earlier, asked the question: "Do you feel accepted by American wives?" Replies from foreign-born wives of both officers and enlisted (with the rank of E-6 and below most strongly represented) included:

"Yes, I feel accepted but I have no friendships."

"People stick by their colors."

"Americans are too arrogant to associate with foreign wives."

"I feel like an outcast."

"Some ladies are very prejudiced against Samoans."

It is so easy for someone not well acquainted with all of the various cultures to say, "Why don't they just band together to help each other out, or meet to seek support from each other in a threatening social situation?" Some Family Support Centers have programs for the foreign-born wives which will bring various ethnic groups together for socials as well as to help with language and job skills. It is difficult to bring together women of different ethnic backgrounds because of deep-seated prejudices. Japanese wives look down their noses at Korean women. Several of them talked during an interview about their husbands' fidelity—if they were sent TDY to another Asian nation. "You never know what happen. Especially if they sent to Korea. Korean girls are, how you say it, more cheap."

The women talked freely of the prejudice between sections of their country. Women from mainland Japan and Okinawan women agreed that the Okinawans did not particularly like the mainland Japanese

★      ★      ★

because: "The Japanese think they are better than the Okinawans. They have so heavily taxed the Okinawans for many years. They took our men to fight their war." On the other side, mainland Japanese women felt that the Okinawans discriminated against them in the case of jobs. As the wife of an Air Force sergeant explained, "I called about a job the other day, and the man could tell that I speak a little different from Okinawan—an accent. He ask if I am Japanese. When I say I am, he tell me that he need no more workers. I know this is because I am Japanese."

## WHEN THE BRIDE IS A PROSTITUTE

As if there were not enough problems inherent in marriage to a foreign national, there are devastating problems that have resulted from "quicky" marriages involving bar girls or prostitutes. Reports from Korea indicate the involvement of organized crime, which continues to use the "brides" in a well-organized prostitution ring after they get to America. Many of the Asian or Pacific Island women met their husbands—the largest percentage of whom are from the lower enlisted ranks at the time of the meeting—in bars. One source estimates that nearly 80 percent of Filipino wives and a large percentage of Korean wives were working in bars or clubs when they met their servicemen husbands. What must be remembered is that the cultures of these women do not always view the status of the bar waitress as Americans do, and for many of these women working in a bar (or occasional prostitution) may be their and their family's only means of support.

Additionally, Bok-Lim C. Kim in her report "Women in Shadows" indicates that near the large military bases there are bars, massage parlors, restaurants, and hotels which "create a subculture into which young girls are drawn seeking work and looking for an American G.I. to marry."

It must also be remembered that many military men find Asian wives through the same channels they do in the United States—

*          *          *

classrooms, mutual acquaintances, church and other social functions. However, for the grades E-4 and below, the most common place to meet Asian or Pacific Island women is still the bar or military club. In Korea, just outside the Air Force base at Kunsan, is Silver Town (formerly A Town), an enclosure of bars and clubs set up chiefly to cater to the needs and desires of the American military man. Also, as on Okinawa, many Filipinos are hired throughout the Pacific on three-month contracts to work in bars and clubs frequented mainly by American servicemen. Of these women, one source who wished to remain anonymous estimates, nearly 90 percent will engage in "hurry-up" marriages with an enlisted man and swell the ranks of Asian-born wives.

"Marriage to American servicemen is big business in Olongapo [the Sin City discussed in Chapter 4]," said Chaplain Metcalf in his paper "Is Love Enough to Make a Marriage?" Based on nine years of studying Philippine/American marriages and six hundred counseling cases, he says, "There are dozens of unscrupulous lawyers, travel agents, marriage agencies, and others who thrive on 'helping' the serviceman to find and marry the right girl. Many merchants along Magsaysay Drive and Rizal Street make money by selling souvenirs, drinks, and time with their girls. These girls are aggressive, beautiful, and very charming. They are professionals at what they do. . . . A business that many of the girls carry on is finding lonely, unsuspecting, and uninformed men of a different culture—American servicemen to marry. . . . The divorce rate is high. According to the Base Legal Office at Naval Station Subic [in the Philippines], 80 percent of marriages contracted between servicemen and Filipino girls end in divorce or annulment within three years."

The reasons, says the chaplain, that the girls come in from the provinces to work in Olongapo include economic security, which often involves getting to the United States; the desire to find a sailor or marine who will send money after he leaves Subic or, better yet, an allotment check (the magic number is about $160 a month, which

**141**

makes a girl rich in Olongapo); and a wish for access to the base at Subic with all its opportunities where a 'hospital only' I.D. card is of great value.

The Navy chaplain also pointed out cultural differences. "The girls of Olongapo may speak very good English, like American music, and dress like Americans, but their cultural backgrounds are very different from [that of American]. . . . On the average, most of the girls working as 'hostesses' in Olongapo have only a sixth-grade education. When they go to the United States this lack of education will adversely affect their sense of self-worth as their ability to find employment or communicate will be limited. The provinces from which they come are rural, and are often impoverished. Their view of what life is and is not has been set and may run counter to [American] expectations. Their religion is Roman Catholic. However, because of the deep historical roots of Malayan culture, . . . their religious views often differ greatly from Roman Catholics in the States. Attitudes are very different in general. Love might be [the American's] reason for marrying a lovely Filipino, but she might see marriage as a means to security in the form of allotment, a trip to the States, or an I.D. card."

Chaplain Metcalf's advice to the young serviceman is to take the time to meet the Filipino people. As he said, there are "many lovely ladies in the Philippines—waitresses, schoolteachers, pharmacists, civil servants, nurses, and doctors. Very few of these women work in Olongapo; most are in Cebu, Baguio, Manila, or the other cities."

NBC News reporter Brian Ross did a two-part report on the Korean slave trade involving wives of American G.I.'s. Korean gangsters, he said, "often force women to work against their will" in the many wide-open houses of prostitution and bars in Houston, one of many cities in which this practice flourishes. The gangsters also have recruiters "who look for the Korean wives of American G.I.'s stationed [in Kansas near a large military base]—women who came to

★                                       ★                                       ★

this country looking for better lives, but whose marriages have failed, or who get in debt, or who, in many cases, worked as prostitutes in Korea to begin with."

Ross also maintained that the prostitution around bases in Korea is going on "with the full knowledge of the American military."

Nationally known columnist Jack Anderson, writing with Dale Van Atta, asserts that 'Military procurement' gets a new definition with the U.S. Army in Korea—prostitution. We recently reported that the Army, by unwittingly allowing bogus GI marriages to prostitutes, is the largest importer of Korean hookers to the United States.

"The Army isn't happy. The top brass doesn't want to be saddled with that reputation. In an eight-page response to our query, the Army paints itself as an overwhelmed police force doing the best that it can. But the best isn't good enough."

"Federal investigators and regional vice police assure us that in recent years, Korean hookers arriving as GI brides have become the most pervasive form of organized prostitution."

Anderson's column cites incidences of some G.I.s marrying as many as four Koreans while stationed in Korea. They could earn $10,000 per marriage. In New York eighty Koreans, working as prostitutes, were arrested following an underground sting operation. All eighty were married to soldiers.

Writing in the *Los Angeles Times*, reporter Paul Feldman noted that in the Los Angeles suburb of El Monte sheriff's deputies raided five businesses "in an effort to break up what [they] described as a local branch of a nationwide network of Korean-staffed houses of prostitution. Young Korean women, often entering the United States under the guise of being wives of military personnel, move from city to city to practice prostitution, Sheriff's Deputy Bill Wehner said. . . . Authorities believe that many of the women enter the country by engaging in sham marriages with American servicemen abroad, who receive up to $10,000 cash to participate."

**143**

## THREATS KEEP THEM IN LINE

For the Western man who married an Oriental girl because he liked the feeling of having power over her, trouble may erupt in the marriage if the wife learns American ways and becomes somewhat more independent. When communication breaks down or total control over the wife is lost, spouse abuse may result. Numerous cases of battering, sexual abuse, extreme neglect, or desertion involving Asian-born wives are reported monthly. It is also very probable that these cases are underreported, as many wives follow a tradition of suffering in silence; others fear that they may be sent home and thus shame their families; some wives have been threatened with deportation by their husbands.

Social workers said that many husbands keep their wives subservient by effectively using the threat of taking away their green cards and having them deported. These wives may not be educated as to the availability of agencies that can help them, or may have been kept isolated from other wives. Asian brides marrying United States servicemen are issued "green cards" (actually blue in color). This alien registration card permits noncitizens to live in the United States as permanent legal residents. (If the military man is only engaged to a foreign woman when he leaves the Orient and wishes to bring her to the States for a visit, a "Fiancée Visa" can be obtained. The couple must go through the same clearance procedures required for getting the green card. However, if the couple does not marry within ninety days, the "Fiancée Visa" will be revoked and the woman returned to her native land.)

As a member of the American Consulate in Japan explained, the husband has absolutely no control over the green card; it can be revoked only if it has been obtained illegally. The card is rendered invalid by fraudulent statements, such as that made by the foreign-born wife who lied about being a professional prostitute on the original application form. Since a large percentage of Asian brides

*                                    *                                    *

may have been involved in prostitution at one time or another, and the husband may have been aware of this, he may use the threat of having the card rescinded. However, a waiver is available in the case of occasional prostitution if the economic situation made this life-style necessary and if the future bride explains this at the time the green card is issued. Sometimes the husband wishes to pursue the charges of prostitution in order to end the marriage, but as the consulate member stated, "If the marriage has survived for some time, it would be hard to prove the charge of professional prostitution. It would be simply his word against hers."

Even a divorce from her American husband does not mean that the Asian-born wife will lose the green card, unless she leaves the United States without immigration permission and remains abroad for one year. As long as she remains in the States and abides by its laws, she can retain her permanent legal resident status. Obviously isolation, inability to communicate, and lack of knowledge regarding American immigration laws may put many foreign-born brides in this blackmail situation with their husbands, with the end result being great psychological abuse.

## WHAT THE MILITARY IS DOING

Since 1950, the military has done an about-face in its attitude regarding military personnel marrying foreign nationals (as it did on enlisted men asking and receiving permission to marry). Until the early 1950s, it was almost impossible for servicemen to get permission from the military to marry Japanese women and bring them home to the United States. Then in 1952, United States immigration laws were revised to allow a greater acceptance of non-Europeans into the United States. While the military gradually relaxed its views and a man could officially marry a Japanese national, the practice was still discouraged. Today, if a man processes the necessary paperwork, little is done officially to stand in his way. However, as one Navy captain stated, "I don't know how many are marrying Asian wives, but it's too damn many! Right now I have a chief and a lieutenant who have requested permission to marry Japanese wives. Legally they can go ahead and do this, but I intend to put every stumbling block I can find in their way. They're not young sailors; they're old enough to know this is not a good thing."

Chaplain Metcalf indicated that for those men requesting to marry in the Philippines, the Navy has a two-page list of items that must be completed prior to the marriage. It includes: visit the Navy Marriage Office, round up birth certificates, take physical exams, upon Navy approval get "Certificate of Legal Capacity to Contract Marriage," apply for a visa, visit (without the intended spouse) chaplain or marriage counseling office to take a look at the problems of interracial and intercultural marriages. The other services basically follow the same routine.

A joint-service regulation on "Marriage in Oversea Commands" clearly stated: "It is the policy of the Departments of the Army, Navy, and Air Force that all active duty personnel have basically the same right to enter into marriage as any other citizens of the United States in the same locality. Armed Forces personnel stationed in or visiting foreign countries are required to obtain written authorization from the senior oversea area commander of their particular branch of service prior to marrying." (Civilian employees are not required to ask permission.) The commanders are instructed to "initiate and complete the investigative checks and examinations necessary to pre-determine the alien's probable admissibility to the United States prior to granting permission to marry."

An alien is barred from admission to the United States if she has problems in one of several areas including mental retardation, drug addiction, and disease (including such contagious ones as chancroid, gonorrhea, leprosy, syphilis, and tuberculosis, or if she is a prostitute or an anarchist.) Said one reporter writing in *Soldiers* magazine, "[The] contagious diseases [category] now includes positive results from a test for AIDS-related human immunodeficiency virus." Supposedly,

*                              *                              *

the charge to the commanders includes a close look at the ability of the young soldier, E-4 and under, to support a spouse.

Certainly the problems facing foreign-born brides, particularly those from Asia, are serious and must be taken into consideration by all involved, including the military. Since it appears that fairly large numbers of these marriages will continue, the military has begun to do what it can to insure stability. Family support centers, at just about every base, offer counseling, including counseling by foreign-born wives. Clubs are formed to bring together wives from specific areas so that they have a network of women with a common language. They assist the new wife in her communication skills, as well as help her establish friendships that help alleviate feelings of isolation. Many of the bases—especially overseas—either offer English-as-a-second-language classes or coordinate with local public high schools who offer such classes. Orientation classes acquaint the newly married woman with American customs. In 1971, the USO established a brides' school program in Seoul, Korea, which was designed to improve intercultural understanding between Korean and American family members. A similar program has also been established on Okinawa. In addition, the military has begun to study the problems facing the foreign-born spouse and her family.

Family service centers can mobilize to help with individual problems. As just one example, Sandra Paige, Director of the Hickam Air Family Support Center, told of a Korean wife of an enlisted man who was assigned to Hickam Air Force Base. The family support center staff was alerted because not only did the wife not speak English, but she had a child with special needs. Before she arrived, center personnel had mobilized the Korean wives' group and the parents of a handicapped children's support group to give her whatever assistance they could.

With all the programs begun these last few years, being a foreign-born wife has been made easier—if the woman herself takes the first step. There are people who want to help at each base but each

★          ★          ★

foreign-born wife must work hard to create her own life in the United States. All must battle the indifference, and even at times, hostility. Accepting foreign-born wives is but one more skirmish of the war on the home front. Help and friendship needs to be extended so that no such wife will ever have to say, "I was so alone."

★            ★            ★

"Had I known the civilian attitude toward employment of military dependents, I wouldn't have bothered. For at the time it was easier to make it as a monotone in the Mormon Tabernacle Choir than it was to be an Air Force wife and be hired as a part-time cashier at a grocery store."

—ANN COMBS,
SMITH COLLEGE NEVER TAUGHT ME HOW TO SALUTE

★  ★  ★

The military wife need not apply. It doesn't matter if she is a foreign-born wife, an ethnic minority, or white. Time after time the military wife is told: "The job is no longer open," "We're hiring from within," "We've made it our policy not to hire military wives," or "Locals only need apply."

Anne, the young wife of an Air Force captain, completed her job application and handed it to the personnel manager of a bank in Rapid City, South Dakota, site of Ellsworth Air Force Base whose hefty annual payroll is spent largely in the community.

"When he saw my husband was in the Air Force, he handed my application back to me and said, 'We don't hire military wives.' He would not keep it on file for future consideration." Anne's story has a positive ending only because she persisted in her job search and eventually was hired by another civilian firm in Rapid City that did not discriminate against military wives.

As the new kid in town the military wife fights four roadblocks: companies hire from the local population, thereby freezing out military wives; promotions are from within, leaving mostly entry-level jobs for military wives as well as other applicants; major bases are located in isolated areas far from employment centers and their employees are mostly local hires; and military brass consistently "suggest" that senior officers' wives not work. (Even after a directive was issued by the Secretary of Defense in 1987, wives continued to report pressure on them not to work.)

For wives of senior officers the real kiss of death to a career is delivered by top brass who order "their" commanders' wives not to

**151**

work or "suggest" they quit jobs to become full-time adjuncts to their husbands' careers. The military has a two-hundred-year-old tradition that officers' wives do not work, and every military manners book in print lectures officers' wives—for the sake of "his career"—on the importance of not working. If Anne's husband had been a more senior officer or a commander, the military would have stonewalled any chance she had at a career. In scores of interviews wives repeatedly said: "I gave up my job when he became commander." "When we joined the wardroom on the submarine my husband's captain suggested it would be better if I didn't work." Dozens of women said: "You can use my story, but please don't use my name; my husband's career will be jeopardized." In the very first interviews that remark smacked of paranoia. How could "they" crush a man or derail a career for what his wife said? Or pressure her to quit work? Hundreds of interviews later, the reality hit that every one of these women had seen careers damaged by commanders who had refused to give commendations or refused to recommend for transfer or promotion. It takes a remarkable woman to defy such pressure, and it is indeed remarkable that two wives spoke out publicly about the injustice.

Trouble in the seemingly tranquil waters of military spousehood began when the *Indianapolis Star* and the *Air Force Times* published complaints from two colonels' wives, Judy P. Croxton and Nataya Leuenberger, about pressure from their husbands' commander of the 305th Air Refueling Wing, part of the Forty-second Division at Grissom Air Force Base in Indiana "to quit their jobs with warnings the careers of their husbands would suffer if they did not. . . . The wives charged it was made clear their husbands would not advance unless they devoted more time to voluntary social and charitable activities at the base."

In May 1985, Colonel Roy D. Croxton Jr., now retired, was nominated to be a vice commander of the Forty-second Air Division. The investigation said "Following Colonel Croxton's nomination . . . the division commander, then Brigadier General Larry Fortner, ad-

*     *     *

vised [Colonel Howard L. Kravetz, the 305th commander] that he would not nominate Colonel Croxton . . . as long as Mrs. Croxton was working." When that edict was communicated to Colonel Croxton, Mrs. Croxton quit her civil service position as manager of the Air Force Suggestion Program at Grissom and thus lost not only her salary but accrued benefits including retirement pay.

Colonel Kravetz was said to have warned Colonel John F. Leuenberger that since his wife decided to continue working full-time it "would probably make [him] noncompetitive for professional advancement." In meeting with the new commander, "Colonel Leuenberger recognized an impasse and brought up the possibility of leaving the command." He was reassigned to a post in West Germany. The question must be asked: Did the wives speaking out result in one husband retiring early as a colonel and the other being transferred to Germany?

What about the commander named by the women in their separate complaints? He was completely exonerated by a military "investigation" because there was no Air Force policy statement on the issue of working wives. At the end of a month-long query into the wives' charges, the Associated Press quoted Major Ken St. John, an Air Force spokesman, as saying, "We found no evidence that there was a violation of any policies, regulations, or law that would warrant disciplinary action."

Because of all the adverse publicity, and after a subcommittee of the House Armed Services Committee interviewed wives in the United States and overseas and confirmed that wives had been told not to work, Secretary of Defense Caspar W. Weinberger signed a letter on October 22, 1987, addressed to the secretaries of the military departments. As quoted in the *Air Force Times*, Weinberger stressed that "spouses . . . have the right to seek employment, to be homemakers, or to volunteer for command-sponsored activities." He further indicated, "No military member will be adversely rated or suffer any adverse consequences from the decision of the member's spouse [to

**153**

*          *          *

seek employment] . . . nor shall a spouse's employment be a consideration in either assignments or promotions."

Nevertheless, because the pressure is still on wives not to work, many military couples are asking, "How can this directive be enforced?" Several wives interviewed after October 22, 1987, have indicated that the word is still out: If your wife works, the command will not be open to you.

There are duties the wife must perform for the command. In fact, an article in the *Air Force Times* states that while top Air Force officials assured wives that holding jobs would not affect their husbands' careers, the officials also emphasized that spouses of commanders and those in key leadership positions are also expected "to participate in activities that support Air Force families." The message seems clear: You have permission to work as long as you also do all that the military expects.

A dinner conversation with an Air Force colonel at an eastern United States base in January of 1989 revealed how some higher-ups plan to respond to the working spouse. "If I have two men with roughly equal abilities up for command, and one wife works and the other doesn't, I'm going to select the man whose wife doesn't work," said the colonel. "I know I can get more from that couple because she will be available for military needs that go with this position." He didn't add, "The Department of Defense directive be damned," but his message came through loud and clear.

An article in the January 2, 1989, *Air Force Times* noted that wives are reportedly still pressured to quit jobs, citing the Women's Equality Action League survey of complaints by Army wives at Fort Stewart, Georgia, about a former commander's wife encouraging them to stop working. The commander's wife supposedly said ". . . 'her girls' didn't have time to do anything but support the military community and their husbands' careers." The article also mentions that a congressional aide reported in December 1988 "that continuing pressure

\*  \*  \*

for the spouses of Air Force officers to abandon their jobs was contributing to the loss of Air Force pilots."

One wife, who had talked to the investigative committee and who asked not to be identified, said that the wife of her husband's boss, a Mrs. General, called her and stated, "Well, of course, my dear, if you don't feel you can handle *your job* [the volunteer duties of an overseas deputy commander's wife], we'll just have to find someone who can." The matter was also mentioned to the woman's husband, a deputy commander.

Another wife whose husband was head of a section in an Air Force support division was called by the division commander's wife in May 1989, and asked if she was telephoning information each month on division coffees and luncheons to "her ladies." When she replied that she was not, the commander's wife said, "Well, you SHOULD BE." The section chief's wife (who is employed) explained that she did send out a monthly memo but that her time was too valuable to spend hours on the telephone to wives who probably didn't want to be called anyway, since none had attended any of the functions. "I think she [the commander's wife] could tell by the very, very cool tone of my voice that I was not happy with her directive. At any rate she backed off, for now." Apparently the pressure to put wifely "military duties" before self-employment or other interests is still very much alive. Many wives have reported being given similar "orders"—long after the directive came out.

As was stressed in Chapter 2, the officer's wife is expected to share her husband's occupation. Her behavior and actions are dictated by the needs of her husband's career. One wife of an Army colonel, who had initially sought employment overseas, changed her mind. "I had worked before we were married and thought I would do so here. However, there are so many social obligations and volunteer projects connected with his new job that I'm not sure I could hold down an outside job and the job of being his wife and hostess."

In an interview, an Air Force colonel's wife stated that her husband

**155**

★                               ★                               ★

had been extremely blunt. "I'm bucking for general," she quoted him, "and your job is to do volunteer work and handle the social niceties that will help me do this. Your working is out of the question."

Many generals have been unwilling to accept a man in the position of commander unless his wife accompanied him. One lieutenant colonel stated that when his wife opted not to accompany him overseas, he was told that he would not be considered for the command. Air Force wives of wing commanders routinely talk of having been interviewed by the general before their husbands were given the position. As was reported by the Associated Press Wire Service, many times wives are bluntly told, either by their husbands or their husbands' bosses, to quit work.

Policy or not, many wives have encountered what Croxton and Leuenberger had complained about. Jolene, married three years to an Air Force colonel, previously had held an excellent administrative position in the Pentagon when her husband got a set of orders. "When we were sent to the Philippines, it was tactfully mentioned to me that I shouldn't work. However, I transferred my civil service seniority and did work as a secretary while we were there. When we left and came here [another overseas posting], I was told by [my husband's] boss that his position meant I could not work. I haven't tried to find a job; I'm sort of considering this as a vacation. Our social commitments and the committees I've been *assigned* to keep me very busy."

A Navy commander's wife who is a successful businesswoman ignored an edict to not work. "The incoming base commanding officer stated at his change of command that 'his' wives would not work. I sort of chuckled. I wouldn't let what he said affect me; no way would I give up my job as a sales rep for one of the Fortune 500 companies. What I do is between my husband and me. However, the commander's message was repeated at hail and farewells as praise for the outgoing wife who devoted her entire life to the Navy and [being] a

★ ★ ★

volunteer for Navy Relief. It's a form of brainwashing I refuse to buy into."

Knowing that a position as battalion commander was imminent, one Army couple took the time to hammer out their roles. They confronted issues that would affect personal and family goals. Writing in the *Military Chaplains' Review*, Carolyn Howland Becraft, chair of the Army Family Action Committee, says, "A significant part of our deliberations involved what would be demanded of me as a commander's spouse. It was well known that many senior commanders refused to accept officers for command positions if they were unmarried or if their spouses would not accompany the officers to the new assignment. In addition, we were aware of the subtle, and sometimes not so subtle, pressure on commanders' spouses not to be employed. Service publications and training materials reinforced the view that a successful commander is one who has a wife to assume the traditional social and volunteer responsibilities in the military community." In spite of the acknowledged pressure, the agreement worked out between them was that they would maintain two households. "The military responsibilities were his; the social responsibilities we would share." Through creativeness, she managed to continue with her professional responsibilities while attending selected military social functions.

But not all wives have the financial resources of Carolyn Becraft. Giving into the brainwashing makes it hard for wives, particularly if their priorities are different from the military's expectations. "I just haven't been able to adjust satisfactorily to not working and having nothing to do that I feel is worthwhile," whispered a formerly employed colonel's wife who asked not to be identified. "I feel as though I have no purpose in life except to entertain for my husband's job, stand by his side at the various functions, or volunteer at family services and the gift shop. I've tried to accept the fact that that is what most military wives have always done, but I've been so upset about this lately that I've had to go see a doctor." She laughed rather self-consciously. "So I guess you can say I'm under a doctor's care."

## GEOGRAPHIC BACHELORS

There are a growing number of wives who are refusing to accompany their husbands or to make "one more move." A geographic bachelor is a term coined to describe an unaccompanied married military man who is living alone at his new duty station because his wife has said, "I won't go." Her reasons for refusing to move include her career, having children established in a good school, or owning a house she doesn't want to leave. But more often it is choosing her career over his. A young, bright woman does not want to give up years of school and a promising future for a succession of low-paying jobs with little chance for career advancement. She is being joined in increasing numbers by the loyal, "good" military wife who is reaching her mid-to-late thirties with a strong desire to establish herself in a career before it is too late. She no longer wants to be free labor, or hold one more low-paying job.

Each military couple must face the dichotomy of a military marriage. In order to promote, he must take assignments that often separate him from his family or move him and the family at least every three years, if not more often. With each career move for him, the wife faces either giving up what she worked so hard to achieve at the present duty station, moving with him and starting over again, or choosing her career over his. If she puts her foot down, what are the choices? A long-distance marriage, with her husband going alone to the next assignment, a decision by her husband to get out of the service, or divorce. A growing number of military men—highly trained at great expense to the government—left in the early 1980s or turned down career assignments because of their wives. Suddenly, the military became concerned with spousal employment.

"It costs the Air Force $1.6 million to train a fighter pilot for the new high-tech F-15 and F-16 aircraft. Yet the number one reason why

&#42;&#9;&#9;&#42;&#9;&#9;&#42;

pilots leave the Air Force is family unhappiness," noted Representative Patricia Schroeder, a Democrat from Colorado, writing in the *Air Force Times*. "The percentage of pilots leaving the service after their first tour recently increased to 40 percent. This is an incredible and expensive drain on our military readiness." Representative Schroeder also called the attitude toward service members and their families the "single biggest threat to our national defense."

Admiral Carlisle A. H. Trost, writing in *Wifeline*, a newsletter sent to Navy wives, said, "We realize the unique and difficult employment situation our Navy spouses face with frequent moves. A recent survey demonstrated that 9.2 percent of married active duty Navy personnel were geographic bachelors and that the number one reason for this decision was spouse employment. This impacts on retention because family separation is the number one reason our people leave the Navy." He went on to comment that military wives have three times the unemployment of civilian wives and that more than 50 percent of Navy spouses work. "You can see why finding jobs for relocated spouses has become a major concern at the Navy's highest levels."

"One of my toughest jobs as a commander here in Japan is counseling young airmen, NCOs, and junior officers whose wives are pressuring them to get out of the service because of the lack of job opportunities for the wife," remarked an Air Force colonel. "The men know if they were back in the States, the wife could hold a good-paying position. These families are finding that it's difficult for a wife to develop her career overseas. The family usually needs the money, and I guess the wife feels she needs the prestige. Still, he's got to keep moving if he wants to get ahead in the service."

"My wife didn't accompany me overseas," an Army major stated. "She had a good teaching job in California and was tenured. We talked it over, and I took the unaccompanied tour of eighteen months rather than the three-year accompanied tour."

"He has his career, I have mine," stated an Air Force wife in an article, "Wives Who Say: I Won't" published in a military wives'

**159**

magazine. A librarian and the wife of an Air Force captain, she lived in Peru, Indiana, with an excellent job, while her husband was stationed at Grissom Air Force Base in Lafayette, Indiana. They may have been in the same state but they saw each other only on weekends. This commute lasted until her husband's eventual transfer to Turkey. She elected to stay behind in her good administrative job. Later, when her husband received orders to Hawaii, she decided to accompany him on that tour. "I sent some fifty letters inquiring about jobs and got nowhere. I came over here with very mixed emotions. I was glad we were together but terrified that half my life was over and that since I was without a job, my career had ended." Ultimately, persistance paid off and she landed a job as a librarian at Wheeler Air Force Base, and eventually at Hickam Air Force Base.

After the second or third move with Uncle Sam, the military wife realizes just how difficult it is to find and keep a good job, especially one with good possibilities for promotion. She knows if she leaves her current position she'll have to start all over again, often in an atmosphere hostile to military wives.

## FIGHTING PREJUDICE

Minorities are protected by law; military wives are not. Each woman must deal with Uncle Sam's longstanding tradition that officers' wives *don't* work, as well as with civilian prejudice against military wives. The laws prohibiting discrimination in hiring do not include discrimination against military wives. Perry S. Patterson, Jr., executive officer of the San Diego Navy Legal Service Office, said, "There is no legal recourse military spouses have. My advice to them is there is nothing you can do about it." Some states carry a "marital status" category on their books, but this law only prohibits discrimination on the basis of whether a person is married or not; it does not prohibit discrimination against those who are married to transient spouses. Military wives have filed discrimination complaints in several states, only to have them rejected. A majority of wives will not

★                                    ★                                    ★

complain because they unfortunately continue to say publicity could damage their husbands' careers.

Discrimination against military spouses comes in many forms. Firms in some military communities have run classified ads that specify, "Locals only need apply." But the exclusion is usually more subtle. Personnel directors and employment agencies have policies not to hire military wives. They screen out military wives by asking the supposedly illegal question: "What does your husband do for a living?" or "What brought you to San Diego?" Employers use these tactics to weed out "transients," saying they lose time and money training a person who stays for a few short months. Military wives say they stay on a job as long as civilians. The average tour of duty is two to three years—the average length of a civilian's employment with one company.

Even civil service, which employs a high ratio of military wives, has forms that ask: What is your husband's DROS (date of return from overseas)? "That's like asking when a civilian will be transferred by Sears & Roebuck," said a substitute teacher in Okinawa.

Sheila, wife of an Air Force major, was asked "How long is your husband going to be stationed here?" when she interviewed for a teaching position in Rapid City. Even though she was upset by the question, she turned it into a positive experience. "It was a sort of group interview with two other women also applying for the position. They were quite a bit younger than I, so I merely looked at the principal who was conducting the interview and said that while he might have to worry about my having to leave the position because my husband might be transferred, he didn't have to worry about me getting pregnant." She got the job.

## MAKING CHOICES

What are the military wife's choices? If his is the primary career and she chooses to follow him, then she must be flexible and aggressive in her job search. Travel may be an advantage to military life but

**161**

★ ★ ★

these frequent moves kill her hopes for a career, job seniority, or accrued benefits. After interviewing scores of wives, it appeared that their options included: starting over at entry-level jobs with each move, taking whatever jobs were available (often out of their career fields and at low pay); putting their careers on hold until their husbands retired; becoming entrepreneurs and creating "portable" jobs; working for civil service, which guarantees a job—only if there is an opening and not necessarily at the same pay grade; or refusing to move with their husbands, which might cost them a command. Most wives avoid a major war on the home front by adopting a secondary role and moving with their husbands.

One career field where some employment can be found is teaching. As a teacher, Sheila has a better chance to be hired than wives in other career fields. She may have a job with each move but it could be substituting and most definitely lacks job tenure and all the other benefits teachers accrue. Military wives feel they work harder trying to prove themselves as did Bonny, a Marine Corps wife, who with her teaching credentials, was always able to find a job—substituting. "We'd move and every August I'd be at the bottom of the substitute list. They'd call people they knew first and it would be October or November before I'd be called. When something happened to a regular teacher I'd substitute full-time, but at half pay. It was always a class no one wanted. Invariably the principal would say, 'You're doing a great job; how would you like to work full-time next year?' I'd go home to celebrate; my husband would have a set of orders."

Nurses, health care professionals, sales clerks, and secretaries usually can find a job, but nearly always at low-paying entry levels. Even with the severe nursing shortage, the status for nurses has not changed. In 1989, an assistant public relations director for a large medical center explained, "We have a large number of military wives working at our medical center. They are at a monetary disadvantage because all new nurses start at Step One. As they are here longer, each earns longevity pay increases through step promotions. Military

★　　　　　　　　　★　　　　　　　　　★

wives are rarely here long enough to earn more than one step promotion. The only nurses to start at higher salaries are those with special training such as pediatric nurses or nurses in ICU [Intensive Care Units] or Critical Care. They require constant updating of their education and their rate of pay is higher initially."

Independent salespeople count on a deficit year or more until they establish contacts. "You don't just walk right into a new community and start selling," said Cynthia, a real estate agent. "I've been here three years and am just starting to get name referrals. But now I'm leaving. I'll be able to carry with me my designation from the nationally recognized Graduate Real Estate Institute, but not my state license, which very few states reciprocate. So I will have to retake the test."

Other wives sell Mary Kay or Avon cosmetics or become dealers for Amway or Tupperware to earn extra money. Others teach classes in aerobics, dance, arts and crafts, foreign languages or dressmaking/ tailoring. Wives who volunteer their services in the numerous family support centers and are given some counseling or receptionist training often find they can land either secretarial or paracounseling jobs. If a wife is versatile, has developed a number of skills, and knows how to sell those skills, she will be more likely to find a job of some sort. For most this may be only a stop-gap measure, but it does enable the wife to keep credentials current, to maintain a positive feeling that she is a vital, worthwhile individual who is adding at least a little to the total family income.

Not all wives have marketable skills, so with all the mobility in their lives, it's not surprising that the unemployment rate for military wives is sometimes triple that of civilians. Lieutenant Colonel Frankie T. Jones, chief of the Air Force family matters branch at the Pentagon, said in a 1989 article in the *Air Force Times*, "Of the 54 percent of Air Force spouses who normally work, the service estimates that 17 percent are unemployed—triple the national average. Most of the joblessness is caused by permanent change-of-station moves."

★ ★ ★

Army wives are facing 25 percent unemployment it was revealed in an annual Survey of Army Families released in 1987. The survey also noted that of those unemployed spouses "almost half of the jobless have given up hope of finding work."

A DOD survey of over 41,000 military spouses showed that the lack of job opportunities was the most frequently mentioned gripe for enlisted wives; for officers' wives it was a close second to the costs of setting up a new residence. "We need the money; that's why I work," stated the wife of a marine gunnery sergeant. "We have three children and his salary simply doesn't go far enough. He turned down one overseas assignment because we were afraid I couldn't find a job. I'm not civil service, so I have to just take what's available on the open market."

For Cindy, taking what was available on the job market meant losing a whopping eleven thousand dollars a year. "When I was in California, I was the office manager. Then I went with my Navy husband (a Lieutenant Commander) to Hawaii. The best job I found was paying ten thousand dollars to start . . . eleven thousand dollars less than I had been making, but I didn't want to just sit home all day. Besides, my salary improves our living standard a great deal. I hope I can transfer my seniority with this company when we are moved back to the mainland."

## LOCKED OUT OVERSEAS

When a wife must work, couples turn down orders for European or Pacific destinations. Why? The devalued dollar, coupled with abysmal job opportunities for spouses overseas, usually means she doesn't work. The military presence aids foreign economies, but United States agreements with foreign nations on who can hold jobs at United States bases favor local nationals. Approximately 175,000 military wives were overseas in 1981, yet only about five thousand appropriated-fund jobs (receiving government money) and six thousand nonappropriated-fund jobs were available to family members.

★                    ★                    ★

Six years later, not much had changed. As just one example, in 1987 the Civilian Personnel Office on Okinawa hired 2,711 local nationals compared to a paltry 271 military family members. DOD wives held only about half of the jobs available with "moonlighting" enlisted men holding most of the others. The only other possible legitimate employment is with American companies with branches overseas. At one base in Australia the only jobs open to wives were tending bar or packing household goods for moves. No office work was available to military wives because complexities in the Status of Forces Agreement between the United States and Australia resulted in all secretarial work being handled by Australians.

Full-time teaching was usually closed to military wives overseas until 1987, when budget restraints opened a few positions to qualified, on-base military wives. Normally, Department of Defense Dependent Schools hired its faculty and chief administrators from the mainland United States, moving them and their families to bases around the world. In 1987, a tight budget led to overseas recruiting of military wives who were already living at bases with job openings. That same year the House passed a bill that would have severely limited these jobs for military spouses by advocating that new teachers be hired from the United States rather than locally. It was defeated through the efforts of the National Military Family Association. In an *Air Force Times* article, Representative Beverly B. Byron was paraphrased as saying that "locally hired spouses should remain the first priority for hiring at defense schools. The spouses make good teachers and bring with them an understanding of the 'unique strains and stresses that a military career puts on the family.' "

Overseas, the only other teaching positions were tutoring or lecturing for colleges offering extension courses at military bases.

And the problem is not solely confined to overseas assignments. "If your husband gets stationed in Hawaii get set to relax," noted a Navy wife. "Jobs are really hard to come by, especially for 'haoles (white foreigner).' If you're not at least part Oriental, you're out of luck.

**165**

There is a great deal of prejudice and discrimination against Caucasians." Even the military commissaries and exchanges in Hawaii overwhelmingly hire Oriental or "local" women—some who barely speak English. Meiko, a foreign-born military wife, talked about the preferential hiring of Orientals in Hawaii. "I know a lot of military wives could not find work in Honolulu, but I didn't have any trouble because I am Japanese. I'm sure I could get job when they couldn't because the Oriental people stuck together and helped each other get hired."

## CIVIL SERVICE: UNCLE SAM AS AN EMPLOYER

Uncle Sam supervises an estimated five million including active duty, reserve, and 1.1 million Department of Defense civilian employees. One third of Civil Service employees—or 340,000—are women. Included in that number are wives of active duty military men who chose Civil Service for job security, continuity of employment, and retirement benefits. Many incorrectly assume that Civil Service automatically guarantees upward mobility. As she moves with her husband, the military wife is guaranteed a job—if one is available—but not necessarily at her present pay grade. She often has to take a lower-paying job just to retain her status. An Air Force wife at Keesler Air Force Base, Mississippi, stated in the *Air Force Times*, "I'm a GS-9 now, but I started all over again here at the bottom of the heap as a GS-4 clerk typist, simply because that's all that was available here in Mississippi. If you don't latch onto something, there just might not be anything at all to latch onto."

Trying to get hired under Civil Service does not always ensure a fair chance at employment either. As one colonel stated, "When I need to hire a secretary, for example, the Civilian Personnel Office sends me a list of ten names of women eligible for the position. If there are more women eligible, I don't see those names unless I make a special request. If I see qualifications in one of the ten women that I like, unlike a civilian firm, I can't interview her unless I also interview

*                              *                              *

the other nine. If I elect to do the interviews, I must submit all my questions to the Civil Service office prior to the interview process to make sure I'm not asking anything that's illegal. It's so time-consuming and so much trouble to do all of this that most of us just pick a name from off the list or promote someone who's already working within our organization. That is very unfair to those new people trying to get jobs, but the Civilian Personnel Office is so paranoid about grievance and so obsessed with its paperwork bureaucracy that it will literally take an act of Congress to make any changes."

Two important changes have been mandated by law making Civil Service more palatable for military wives. The first change was Executive Order 12632 signed by President Ronald Reagan in May 1982. It "enables spouses of U.S. government personnel who work a total of twenty-four months in overseas positions . . . to receive direct appointments to competitive Civil Service positions when they return to the United States." The second was the Military Family Act (Public Law 99-145), which authorized "the president to order measures considered necessary to increase employment opportunities for spouses of members of the armed forces. The act also requires the Secretary of Defense to prescribe regulations implementing hiring preference for spouses of military personnel in accordance with the law and the president's measures." One of the resulting changes was the Spouse Preference Program. The military wife must apply for such status, which is applicable for six months after a Permanent Change of Station. If all the criteria is met, selection of a spouse eligible for preference is "mandatory if (1) preference has been requested for the vacancy being filled, (2) spouse is among the best qualified candidates, and (3) when the grade of the vacancy is no higher than a grade previously held by the spouse in a permanent, competitive service position." The ruling is not perfect and there is opposition to such preference from "local" Civil Service personnel who are in competition with military wives for each opening. (Unfortunately, it may not be working, for an *Air Force Times* article stated,

**167**

". . . a recent DOD report showed that only twenty-six military spouses have managed to get government jobs through a two-year-old law that is supposed to give them Civil Service hiring preference.")

## UNCLE SAM'S JOB BANK

"The issue of spousal employment is of critical importance to the military because it affects the retention of highly trained men in the armed forces," said Assistant Secretary of Defense Lawrence J. Korb in a 1982 speech in observance of a federal women's program. Solving spousal employment has become every bit as important to retention efforts as reenlistment bonuses and future retirement checks. Obviously these problems of the unemployed or underemployed military spouse are not going to just disappear. If more and more wives become unwilling to follow the tradition of being merely a husband's appendage and say, "It's my time now; I won't go," military family stability will decline. If a solution is not found to the problem of discrimination regarding hiring military spouses, wives will continue to mourn the lack of equal opportunity for employment. What is being done?

Beginning in 1982, in an attempt to retain career professionals, the military began establishing job banks or job information referral systems. A 1987 study said 40 percent of officers' wives and 53 percent of enlisted men's wives reported employment services were available at their bases. According to the DOD Family Policy office, a total of 268 such centers were in operation by the end of 1987.

Some job centers combine the hiring activities of the Civilian Personnel Office for government jobs, the nonappropriated-fund hiring activities, the hiring for exchange services, and listing for many private sector jobs. Some centers also offer workshops on résumé writing, filling out application forms, and interviewing for jobs. These centers can best help wives reentering the job market and women seeking "just a job." Spouses indicate that a major drawback of the spouse employment centers is that they typically list only lower-level

★                                    ★                                    ★

(and lower-paying) jobs. It must also be understood that these centers are *not* employment agencies; they do *not* compete with state agencies or private employment concerns; they *cannot* create jobs where none exist. They do not send wives out to be interviewed for a job; the wife must make her own applications. These centers exist only to give the military spouse helpful tips in seeking employment and to provide lists of positions available in a given area.

The employment centers are in great demand. During 1985, Fort Belvoir, Virginia, spouse employment center assisted 5,231 spouses, from all branches of the armed services, with job referrals or help-sharpening job skills, and helped another 9,767 by telephone. Several months before the center at Pearl Harbor, Hawaii, was in operation in 1986, personnel had received stacks of applications from women looking for work. In an interview, the late Pat Chong Mahaffey, director, indicated that a goal of the center was to be able to provide job listings via computer so a military wife could get her résumé/credentials ready in advance. When the system was fully operational it would help the military man decide what choice of assignments he should accept based on availability of employment for his wife.

An October 2, 1986, order signed by President Ronald Reagan benefited a great number of wives for it gave military spouses hiring preference for the more than two hundred thousand worldwide nonappropriated-fund jobs on military bases. While these jobs as cashiers, child-care workers, and librarian assistants are low paying, they open needed job opportunities to a greater number of wives. A more recent policy change allows employees to be reinstated without a break in service when moving from one nonappropriated-fund job to another within six months. This latter change could solve the problem of "gaps" in work records for many military wives.

On the positive side, these directives surely must enhance military wives' employment opportunities. Life would become better for military wives if more women would speak out about unfair pressures on them not to work. Unfortunately, a career in the military will always

**169**

mean mobility. There is no way Uncle Sam can place job priority for military wives before military readiness. Each woman/couple has to decide how to best meld two careers. The newly established job centers will help young wives as well as women reentering the job market. The job centers with computer hookups with other military bases to enhance job placement for her ahead of a career move for him looks good—especially on paper.

Some solutions to the dilemma of unemployed military spouses are possible. While foreign nationals now employed at overseas bases in exchanges, commissaries, self-help stores and so on might not like the idea, perhaps agreements between the United States and foreign governments could be updated to allow for a greater percentage of employment of military spouses. Many Civil Service and DOD teaching positions could be made available to on-site military spouses instead of importing additional American civilians into an already overcrowded job market. And on the home front, legislation needs to be forthcoming to prohibit discrimination against the mobile military spouse.

On the other hand, spouses should not assume that a job will be provided for them. They must make themselves marketable. For example, Kim and Terry, wives of an Army officer and an enlisted man, are completing college degrees and upgrading teaching certificates in preparation for employment opportunities. Catherine, a Coast Guard wife, is completing a nursing degree so that "I can work while he's still in and when he retires." An Army wife at Fort Monroe, Virginia, who had been told by the local school system that it preferred to hire "local teachers who were more stable" started a catering service. Now on her way to Germany, she says, "At least I can take my business with me, even though I'll have to start over and build a reputation." Other military spouses could learn to be just as resourceful.

One thing is certain: the military will continue to be concerned with the problem of spousal employment because of the profound

★          ★          ★

effect the lack of jobs has on recruitment and retention. So in the future look for more money and focus on spousal employment. It will take a few more years to ascertain if these initiatives will make a difference or be merely a Band-Aid on the festering sore of military wife unemployment and underemployment.

"They call me Mr. Mom," explained the husband of a Coast Guard lieutenant. "I'm beginning to get used to it."

★                          ★                          ★

I n the quietest part of the afternoon when babies sleep and playgrounds don't echo with the sounds of children home from school, James, a retired Navy chief petty officer, sat on the floor of his quarters in Navy housing diligently embroidering layettes for Navy Relief.

In the other room slept a darling little three-year-old girl adopted by James and his wife, an active duty chief, one of the three hundred women deployed on the AR-8 Jason, a heavy haul repair ship, on its six-month WESTPAC run. And to be perfectly precise, since James was now retired from the Navy, he was sitting in *her* quarters in military housing because she was now the active duty military member. She was his sponsor. After twenty years in the Navy, James had switched roles, making him the Navy dependent.

James had adapted well to being a dependent "wife." He was the first male member—and only one at the time of the interview—of the CPO Wives' Club at Pearl Harbor, Hawaii. After he joined, it became the CPO Spouses' Club. At one time he was the only man to belong to the Interisland Coordinating Council of Enlisted Wives' Clubs made up of all enlisted wives' clubs on Oahu. Admittedly, by 1986 the heyday of wives' clubs was past, for there were only 360 members in all the enlisted wives' clubs on the island. In the 1960s, half that number would have been in one club. In 1987, each club was lucky to have twenty members. Nevertheless, the CPO Wives' Club took him in as a member and eventually made him their president—which is better than what the Navy Wives' Club of America did. They took his money, sent his membership to Washington, D.C., and after seven months of debate sent his money back with a "Sorry, we don't accept men." A decidedly biased judgment at a time when the Navy brass issued orders to treat women in the Navy as equal—but not spouses who were men.

"I was upset. Now recently Washington said they'd accept husbands as associate members. But you can't hold office," said James, not missing a stitch. "I joined the wives' club not because I wanted to be the first man but because I needed things to do. The club pays for baby-sitting for club functions and gives me a chance to get out of the house. The CPO Wives' Club has social events and goes out to lunch. I enjoy baking for the bake sales. One wife showed me how to sew. I sewed up a storm. I had fifteen hundred volunteer hours in Navy Relief and thirteen hundred hours making layettes. I used to have worries and stress and migraines when I was in the military. The military is a stressful job. Rigid discipline. But I don't have headaches anymore. My wife does! As much as she tries to not show the tension of her work, she experiences it."

James retired when it became obvious how many problems they'd have getting orders together. Their first move together was to Cutler, Maine, "a cold and isolated place," he says, "but with good fishing. I felt strange at first. I figured that my role as a house husband was to do everything I expected of her if she was home all day. Most of the men thought I was a wimp for not working. When we got here, one kid, whose wife was on the Navy ship USS *Jason*, had just gotten out of the service. She stayed in; he had the pink I.D. card. We bowled the same night. He asked: 'Do you scrub floors and wash toilets? I ain't going to do that. She can when she gets home.' He considered them female jobs. He should have stayed in the Navy and she should have gotten out. He wanted the best of both worlds. I asked him how he liked being a dependent. 'I ain't a dependent,' he yelled back. She finally threw him out."

In today's military, there are growing numbers of civilian men married to female military members. There are more than 223,000

\*　　　　　\*　　　　　\*

female officers and enlisted personnel on active duty or at various service academies—10.3 percent of the military force. The Air Force, as a further example, has almost seventy thousand female members with nearly half of them married. An estimated nine thousand women are married to civilians and the remainder have married another service member, creating dual military-career families. At times both the male "dependent" and the active-duty "wife" run afoul of military traditions and society's stereotypes.

## HOUSE HUSBAND

The military house husband is still enough in the minority to be an interesting phenomena. Like his female counterpart, he is a dependent at the mercy of the military system. As far as the military goes, he becomes a nonperson. It is his wife's Social Security number he must recite for medical records, base library cards, even for housing. All of the base functions are under her name and rank as are the telephone and club card. (If he's retired military, he has his own I.D. and club card.) When she gets a set of orders, it is he who must follow and make do at the next base. Male "dependents" interviewed have the same problems finding jobs as the women discussed in the chapter on work.

"My wife already has PCS [Permanent Change of Station] orders to Hawaii," said the husband of an Army sergeant in her seventh month of pregnancy. His two daughters, one seven and one five, hung on the arms of his chair as he talked. "It appears that she will have to go ahead of me and the two girls, and we'll follow a few weeks later. If the baby is born before she has to leave, I'll just have to cope with formula and diapers, as she can't take the baby with her. The neighbor women all call me 'Mr. Mom,' so I guess I can manage like the other moms do."

While most of the military house husbands realized that they were still in the minority and that society viewed them as being outside the norm, most had handled the problems of day-to-day living fairly well.

**175**

★                                    ★                                    ★

Generally they found that if civilians or other military were at first surprised about the reversal of male/female roles, the novelty quickly wore off. Several did mention that civilians particularly would ask the rather personal question, "Why don't you go into the military and let your wife out?" as if the wife were fulfilling a commitment to her country her husband didn't wish to honor.

There is difficulty fitting into the military social structure for a nonmilitary male. As Mark, whose wife is an Air Force sergeant, explained, "The military is a closed society, especially when you live on base. In one sense it is like being a G.I. without all the problems of being in the military. But when I wasn't working, I felt like an oddball. It is hard trying to carry on a conversation with someone who is in the military if you don't know what they are doing, what is current, and what is going on. If I wasn't working I would really be out of sync. I could see how depressing it would be to be a housewife sitting home alone for days at a time."

When Mark and his wife first got married, he had decided to leave the military. He had his full G.I. bill so he used the time to start work on his college degree at her next assignment in New Mexico. As many women have found, being married to a military person often means not finishing college in one place. He finished work on his degree at her next duty station. Just after graduation he was to begin a promising job as a cartographer when—you guessed it—another set of orders came in.

"This last move put my career on hold. There wasn't much of a call for cartographers in Hawaii so I eventually found a job with the Air Terminal Operations as a dispatcher using my prior Air Force experience. It's kind of a step backward because I had gotten out of the Air Force, earned my degree, now here I am back doing what I did in the Air Force. However, the biggest plus for me is getting to live in areas I never would have seen. My friends stayed in Wisconsin with their homes and mortgages while I've been all over Europe."

Doug, a Ph.D. married to an Army captain, took a leave of absence

★ ★ ★

from his tenured faculty position at an eastern college to accompany his wife to her new assignment in Korea. He indicated that he was willing because he felt his wife ". . . needed to pursue her career at this time," and mentioned that he was looking forward to the experience of living in a different culture. Since the captain could not have her dependents join her until housing was available, Doug was also coping with the job of being the primary parent to the couple's young daughter.

While Mark and Doug were very upbeat in the interviews, they covered rather quickly the chief complaint of all "dependent" spouses interviewed: the difficulty of finding jobs and sustaining a career—the same problems encountered by female spouses. With role reversal, it is now the husband who must sacrifice a career. Whoever makes the sacrifice often uses this as a weapon in the marriage. It becomes the "Look what I had to give up for you" ploy.

Kenneth, husband of an Army staff sergeant, said, "I had a really good job when we were stationed on the East Coast making over twenty-four thousand dollars a year. Now here in Hawaii I'm working as a gardener, making around ten thousand dollars. It's caused some real problems in our marriage as I'm not the real wage earner. I always know I'm living on her money."

One Air Force captain interviewed was very frank in her disclosure that the moves her career required ended the marriage. "My husband moved with me for my previous two assignments. Then he got established in the real estate business in Colorado Springs. When I got orders, he said he would join me later. He hasn't. I went back for a visit a couple of months ago, and he came out here once. But he didn't want to continue to move around. We really don't have a marriage any-more." They have since divorced.

Like many dependent wives, dependent husbands are beginning to say a boisterous "no" to giving up careers. This means that female military members are facing the same basic problems faced by male geographic bachelors. They face either living alone while their husbands stay at the last duty station where they had a good job or making the decision to get out of the military. In addition, since the military is still not considered a traditional career for females, some spouses are still tied to the culture's ideas of accepted male/female roles—it is the wife who follows her husband's job. A married female marine first lieutenant said, "I'm overseas on a one-year unaccompanied tour because my husband finally got a fairly good position in California and didn't want to leave it. He's followed me to two other assignments, starting over each time. This time we decided he should stay in the States." Asked what she planned to do if he again refused to relocate at the end of her tour, she replied, "I guess I'll get out. I can't ask him to keep making those sacrifices. It would be easier for me to follow him since that's the way our society is set up."

The husband of an Air Force captain expressed his doubts at being able to cope with his work situation much longer. " I know she's got a good job and a good pension coming later, but I'm not sure I can stick it out. Man, you wouldn't believe the jobs I've held recently. I'm always able to find some kind of work, but I don't make [any] money at all. It's hard to sit back and see that you aren't going to be able to get anywhere, get a career started like she's done. Then when we have to move, and I can't find work for a few months, we fight because she's the one making and controlling the money. I'm the one who's dependent."

## WHEN BOTH BELONG TO UNCLE SAM

There are 223,000 women in the four branches of the military and about 11 percent of all military families have dual military-career spouses. Usually these spouses are both enlisted or both officers, for the military frowns on fraternization, but some couples do cross the rank barrier. The lives of these dual-career military families differ greatly from those led by typical civilians. Both husband and wife have demanding, time-consuming occupations with duty hours that often stretch into twelve-hour shifts, seven-day alerts, or three-month

★　　　　　★　　　　　★

patrols. All too often it is the wife who will be like so many other American women who contribute to the family income while having the added responsibility of taking care of children. In the military she must share child care for she may be a navigator on an Air Force tanker or aboard a seagoing vessel repairing equipment. Like her husband, she has her job and her orders, which, like his, must take precedent over family matters.

When the traditional roles are overturned, who keeps the home fires burning? Somehow, both have to cover for each other. Many of the couples interviewed said the husband had the "nine-to-five" job in the military that permitted him to be the primary parent. What makes it difficult for both in a dual military marriage is the excessive demand on their time: military duties added onto "regular" jobs, their separate prolonged absences, and child care problems.

In the event of a war or an alert, parents cannot say to Uncle Sam, "Sorry, I can't go. I have to baby-sit." For many couples, good child care is the biggest issue. So both active duty military members (like the single military parent) must file a detailed dependent care plan that states specifically who is going to care for the child/children when they are deployed to the field or sent on a mission. Obviously it can't be the teenager next door, for often the call to test readiness of a unit comes in the middle of the night. There has to be a competent adult willing and able to baby-sit at all hours.

"My husband was flying, and my group had a recall about two in the morning," explained Patrice, an Air Force captain. "We were new to Kadena Air Force Base [Okinawa], and I hadn't had time to locate a sitter for nighttime. Finally I became so frantic that I simply walked next door, woke this woman whom I had never met, explained my problem, and asked if she would keep my son. I think she was rather overwhelmed but she agreed, and we became fast friends. She let me file her name for emergency care and has helped me out any number of times when my husband was TDY and I had night duty. But I don't know what I would have done if this woman had refused."

★                    ★                    ★

A civilian couple frantically searching for any warm body to baby-sit—and ideally a competent one—knows how desperate the situation of child care can be for social engagements, much less for work on a daily basis. Take any and all problems civilian parents have finding and keeping child-care givers and compound the problem military parents have with long hours and mobility. Find a competent care giver and count the days until her husband's set of orders means searching once again for someone competent.

One sergeant, whose wife was TDY to Alaska, handled his erratic life-style by bundling up their sleeping daughter and at 3 A.M. taking her to their regular baby-sitter who lived close by in the same housing area. "I told the sitter I'd be back by midmorning, but I didn't pick up our daughter until the next day when the alert was called off. And I couldn't even call the baby-sitter to let her know. Fortunately she was an Air Force wife whose husband was called up for the same exercise. A civilian might have panicked when I didn't call or return for over twenty-four hours."

In many cases, both must somehow cover for each other. "I do 80 percent of the parenting," states a major, whose wife, Sondra, is a navigator in the Air Force. "Fortunately as an air traffic controller, I have a more normal work schedule, which allows me to be home with the baby, seven-month-old Nathan. "Also, we have a dependable sitter who comes to the house. People comment about always seeing me with Nathan and never Sondra. But she's flying several times a week, on alert for seven days at least once a month. I have to take over. I don't mind. We've discussed it often, and so far, everything seems to be working out okay."

## CHILD CARE ON BASE

There is, of course, some on-base nursery care—if you can get it. There are more than 639 child-care centers throughout the military caring for an average of 129,000 children a day. Forty-six thousand children are cared for in private homes on base. Even with the growth

★                              ★                              ★

of home care, the DOD estimates a need to care for eighty-one thousand more military dependents. While base nursery hours of operation differ at each base, most offer daylight-into-late-evening care—but this is not long enough to meet the needs of active duty military. Additionally, most child-care facilities have long waiting lists. Bergstrom Air Force Base in Texas, with a capacity to serve only 186 children, at one time had 180 names on a waiting list. The combined facilities of Naval Air Station North Island and Imperial Beach near San Diego can serve only 176 children and limits its waiting list to only ten names per age group. At Camp Pendleton, Oceanside, California, with more than five child-care centers, there were one thousand names on a waiting list, which often means some parents must wait up to a year to obtain child care in a base nursery. It is estimated that this shortage of child-care facilities could last five years or more.

And unfortunately the crunch could continue even longer. Karen R. Keesling, assistant secretary of the Air Force for manpower and reserve affairs, told the House Armed Services military personnel and compensation subcommittee on April 13, 1989, that "the service [Air Force] faces a $102 million shortfall in child-care funding in fiscal 1990." The needs of the military must come first, she noted in an *Air Force Times* article. "Given the budgetary environment in which our bases are operating, we cannot constrain our commanders' use of operational funds. . . . Our commanders have to have the flexibility to apply their scarce resources to the most demanding requirements and priorities. When there is a funding crunch, the planes must still fly."

With the passage of the Military Family Act on November 8, 1985, base commanders have the option of allowing Family Day Care Homes Programs to function on base. Since then growth of home care for children has been phenomenal. Providers of child care are certified by the base and licensed by the state in which the base is located. Home care is one more way for military wives to earn money and has

★                                    ★                                    ★

the advantage of more attention for the child and certainly more flexibility of hours for the parents. Yet, again, there are many long waiting lists.

The DOD issued new guidelines in 1989 to standardize child care, including the home-care givers. While each state differs in local laws, the military directive now includes screening potential providers of care for criminal or mental instability, drug or alcohol abuse; setting a minimum age of eighteen and requiring that they be English-speaking; establishing a monitoring system, and requiring home care providers to be trained in first aid, child development, health, and safety.

Home care offsets some of the shortfalls of nursery care. It must be remembered that base nurseries primarily cater to those women seeking short-term care, a few hours while they go to the commissary or attend a wives' club function. Generally speaking, the military has assumed that most military spouses will not work, and the child-care centers are not designed to meet the needs of the working spouse who must have child care available for extended daytime hours, shift work, or emergencies.

Whether civilian or military, child care is costly. DOD statistics show that while civilian commercial care facilities charge between sixty dollars and one hundred and twenty dollars per week per child, typical military child-care center rates range from thirty-five to fifty dollars per week, per child. Even the military rates create a financial burden for some ranks, but DOD regulations specify that local base commands must set the rates so that fees paid by parents will cover at least two-thirds of the center's operating costs. Fort Ord, California, used a sliding scale based on household size and gross family income to determine payment; still, a typical military family with four or five members, earning fifteen hundred dollars or less per month, can reasonably expect to pay one hundred forty-seven dollars a month for the first child, ninety dollars for the second child, and seventy-nine dollars per month for additional children. Since cost is the same for

*                                    *                                    *

an enlisted or officer's child, rank seldom becomes a factor in child-care rates, but the enlisted personnel's lower salary makes child care a greater financial burden. To date, only the Army is allowing reduced payments for lower-ranking service families, although one Pentagon official disagreed with this policy. "Unless you are going to be providing second-class service for a second-class fee, I don't like the idea of having separate fees."

Assuming that parents are successful in placing their children in military child-care centers, there are still several major problems to be faced. No base nursery will accept a child who is running even a low temperature, for the nursery does not wish to run the risk of infecting other children. However, both parents *must* report for duty. Having a sick child or one who must be taken to the emergency room does not excuse parents from reporting to work. Most dual-career military parents must rely on home care providers or baby-sitters who will come to the parent's home if the child has a slight cold and temperature.

Base nurseries are not a solution for parents wanting more than just minimal child care. Most often the child is safe but receives little individual care because of the large numbers of children in ratio to care givers. Row after row of infants lie in separate cribs receiving attention only when they cry. Make no mistake, these children are not normally abused, battered, or beaten—they are just given minimal care. Most base nurseries do not offer either directed play or a preschool learning environment. They are designed simply for custodial care. The care givers are normally military wives who are paid minimum wage to just watch the children. Nurseries do not require these care givers to have degrees in early child development or any training at all. Toddlers and young children fare a little better because they can socialize in play with each other and on outdoor equipment.

A female Air Force lieutenant surveyed the base nursery as a possible child-care site when she first arrived at her new base. "There were about thirty kids in this one big room, sort of aimlessly playing,

**183**

★ ★ ★

while two women sat at a table in the corner drinking coffee. Oh, the place was fairly clean and the kids weren't beating up on each other, but there certainly wasn't any direction to their play, no learning going on. We didn't know what to do, but through the church we were finally able to get a nice older woman who comes to our home, and she does teach Candy her nursery rhymes."

Military parents have to be just as vigilant as civilian parents in selecting child-care facilities. Children's safety is a factor that has to be considered. A 1987 *Air Force Times* article stated, "Some facilities used by the military as child-care centers may pose a threat to the safety of children because they are old and do not have basic fire protection." Thirteen centers at eight United States military bases were housed in wooden structures with a lack of sprinkler systems and a lack of, or blocked, emergency exits. Some structures date back to World War II. Waivers to the fire code permit these centers to continue operating if the violations are not "life-threatening and if they can be repaired with local funds or if replacement or renovation . . . is scheduled within the next five years." Centers with fire-code violations make up approximately 20 percent of the service's 287 child-care centers.

The military is not immune to the same sex abuse charges that have plagued civilian day-care centers. Reporter P. J. Budahn noted that an unidentified Army spokesman said, "Three pre-schoolers who attended a child-care facility at the Presidio of San Francisco have been confirmed as having venereal disease, and up to seventy more have received counseling for possible child abuse." Two parents filed suit against the government after two three-year-olds were allegedly sexually abused while in a day-care center at Scott Air Force Base in Illinois. In a separate incident on the West Coast parents became aware that their children were being sexually abused in a day-care facility on a Navy base. An investigation followed after the parents filed suit but a judge dismissed the charges. However in the case of Scott Air Force Base, reporter David W. Givans noted, "Since the

*　　　　　　　*　　　　　　　*

alleged incidents, base officials said, a television monitoring system has been installed at the center and new employees are screened through local and national agencies. Employees cannot start work at the center until both the local and national screenings, which take between six and eight weeks, are complete. The center also now [in 1988] requires two child-care providers to be present with the children at all times."

The cases of abuse add to the concerns of parents attempting to find competent care for their children. When child care cannot be adequately solved through private or base child-care facilities, the only option left is for one military member to leave the service. Usually it has been the female service member who has gotten out.

Trying to be a good parent at the same time as meeting all military obligations is not easy, as an academy graduate explained in the *Air Force Times*. She left the service after her five-year commitment was ended because it "became increasingly difficult to devote the time the job required and raise her two young sons. . . . It really is too hard to do both jobs [well]." Her husband, an F-4 pilot, stayed in.

An Air Force couple stationed in Japan realized that the availability of a mama-san (the name for local female sitters) made it possible for both to do their jobs. "We can call her day or night for emergencies, and she will stay at our home until we return. I don't know what we will do when we are sent back to the United States," said the wife, who was a captain. "We probably can't afford to hire a live-in sitter there. I guess one of us will simply have to resign our commission, and I'm sure I'll be the one to do that."

That same sentiment was expressed by an Air Force captain, who said that if she has to make a choice between her family and her career, her decision would be easy. "Only one person can take care of my kids—me. . . . That importance is overriding."

In fact, in 1988, an Air Force Blue Ribbon Panel noted that "In every group of military women the panel talked with, many of those who were married told of being actually encouraged to separate from

*                                    *                                    *

the Air Force to better support their military husbands. The underlying assumption was that a husband's career was primary and would suffer unless the wife was a participative Air Force spouse."

When an Army specialist was prohibited by regulations from having her husband and child join her in Korea, she requested a discharge indicating that she ". . . did not think she should be away from her child during the year-long assignment." Recommendations from an Army social worker, a battalion chaplain, and her company commander that the discharge be granted had little effect until she filed a lawsuit and took her case to the media.

## TOGETHER—EVER AGAIN?

For dual-career couples, and especially those with children, accepting separate tours of duty is a hard decision to make. It is a very real problem because most military couples spend several months to several years apart while awaiting joint assignments. With more and more married couples in the military, it is becoming harder to find joint assignments. Additionally, the higher in rank a couple goes, the fewer the joint choices become.

"They were sending my husband to graduate school and they wanted to send me to Korea," said an Army captain. "That was not something that we were going to accept. . . . Either the Army was going to let us get back together, or we were sincerely talking about getting out."

Many couples feel as they do. If both don't leave, at least one of the military members does. However, some couples feel they can remain in the military as dual-career families, even if they are geographically separated. Another dual-career couple said they had discussed what their actions would be if they were not able to be assigned to the same base. He had reasoned it all out. "I've been in longer than my wife, so if we can just hang in until I reach my twenty years for retirement, I'd retire and let her finish her career. I'd go where she was sent and

★                                    ★                                    ★

not worry about it. Our new assignment is at the same base in Georgia, so we can hope things will continue to work out over the next few years."

Just after having her second child, Denise, an Air Force captain, said, "So far I've managed. My husband helps a great deal when he's not flying. I have a desk job which does not require a great deal of TDY travel. We're doing okay so far, but I can't say for sure what would happen if we didn't have a joint assignment. I guess we'd try to work things out. We both are working hard to make successful careers for ourselves in the military."

Some do work things out. In the report "Families in Blue," the Air Force indicates that perhaps because of mutual choice of arrangements, economic stability, Air Force ability to maintain joint assignments, and mutual fulfillment from their jobs, "Couples in which both the husband and wife are Air Force members are more likely to be happily married than couples with a civilian wife." The report does go on to say, however, that ". . . roughly one out of five dual-military couples are experiencing low marital quality . . . [due to poor] marital communication and sexual intimacy, unsatisfactory companionship, and low levels of mutual confidence and trust." Of course, these marital problems can affect the job performance of both members, but the Air Force feels confident that work and family commitments can be reconciled and that the force may benefit from these dual-career marriages ". . . if it can continue to provide the necessary joint assignments."

With continued hints of reenlistment problems in the all-volunteer military, the Air Force at least is encouraging dual-career couples to stay in. Advertisements in military magazines portray two smiling sergeants, who point out the advantages of career development, retirement benefits, medical care, educational opportunities. All this ". . . added up. We reenlisted . . . look forward to rewarding careers while serving our country."

★ ★ ★

## Putting Teeth into Equality

It was a long haul to convince the military that women were equal, that they had a right to serve their country in the military. It was not an easy battle—nor is it over. In many cases the female service member continues to be treated only as a wife who must fulfull not only her military duties but additionally the duties described earlier of a "good military wife." She is expected to provide goodies for bake sales and help with OWC functions, say many active duty service members and wives. One female captain explained the double standard: "In my squadron, I'm not a 'wife,' just a military member, the same way a man is just a military member. Still, the wives of my squadron see me as just another female. They invite me to their get-togethers and expect me to volunteer my time to help them in their projects. At the same time, I am a 'wife' in my husband's squadron, so I attend those wives' functions and volunteer my time. I am expected to do double duty. Lately, I've been insisting that when there is a military function for my squadron, my husband attend with me just as I have to attend his with him." While a military career is now possible for both single and married women, it seems they still have to overcome these ages-old stereotypes.

Far more serious than the social or familial expectations, however, are the denial of many career-enhancing jobs, the sexual harassment by males at work, and the attitudes of some of the wives of the men active duty females work with. According to some Navy wives "they [active duty females] have taken away the shore duty billets, and the Navy doesn't send them to sea, so it makes it harder for my husband to have a shore billet and time at home."

In an effort to address these concerns, the Navy appointed an officer in the early 1980s to serve part-time as head of women's policy under the Chief of Naval Personnel. The purpose of the job was to oversee "women's progress in obtaining career-enhancing billets" at a time when women were complaining of sexual harassment and being

★ ★ ★

denied promotions. In 1988, a female naval captain, Captain Kathleen D. Byerly, was named as full-time head of the office.

The same year the Air Force opened two thousand support aircrew positions to women that had previously been closed to them by military regulations and federal law barring women from combat jobs. Included were "the two thousand support aircrew jobs, two thousand jobs in Marine Corps security forces, and an undetermined number of jobs in forward Army units. Not included in these totals are nine thousand jobs in Navy reconnaissance planes and supply ships, which Navy officials recently opened to women."

In February 1988, Principal Deputy Assistant Security of Defense for Force Management and Personnel David J. Armor announced a new standard for judging jobs that should be open for women. The importance of the standard is that it does not just apply to one service but has a DOD-wide impact. "From now on . . . the armed services should close a job to women only when the job carries a risk of exposure to direct combat, hostile fire, or capture 'equal to or greater than' the risk for similar units in the same theater of operations."

Representative Beverly B. Byron, chairwoman of the House Armed Services subcommittee, was quoted in the *Air Force Times* as calling the new assignment policy "an important first step" toward fair conditions for military women. "This is a bright report. Let's only hope that it continues as bright as it seems," said Byron. In the same article, Representative Patricia Schroeder of Colorado was quoted as saying the new policies sounded wonderful. "But what I think we can't measure in this hearing is what kind of aggressiveness we're going to have out of the Secretary of Defense on these issues."

The Department of Defense is also said to be taking other steps to reduce sexual harassment and make other improvements for women although as recently as 1987, headlines in the *Pacific Stars and Stripes* indicated that a Navy officer had been found guilty of sexual harassment. A study by the executive committee of the Defense Advisory Committee on Women in the Services indicated that women overseas

**189**

usually had more problems than those stationed in the United States, with the Pacific being targeted as hardest hit by sexual harassment. The report specifically cited incidents occurring aboard the salvage ship USS *Safeguard* where the captain struck a female crew member on the buttocks with his hand, "offered to 'sell' female sailors on his vessel to Koreans, and [did] nothing to stop sexual harassment . . . on his ship."

Representative Schroeder also commented on this issue, indicating that she felt the military did not always thoroughly investigate charges of sexual harassment. "With sexual harassment, I remember chaplains and different base commanders telling me the problem was if they reported incidents on their bases, it went on their records that they were not running the bases well. So the incentive was to cover it up and not deal with it."

On the other hand some progress may be occurring in individual cases. One Navy chief recounted, "The Navy *makes* the Navy treat my wife equal. One guy said no female chief would be allowed in the chief's mess. The master chief of the command had a talk with him. 'You can't be that way. You have to accept females or at least appear to accept them. If you won't change your attitude—get out.' The man retired."

This is just one incident among many. Unfortunately, the military continues to encourage the "macho" male image that, as the Defense Advisory Committee stated, "is at best inappropriate and at worst morally repugnant."

As the all-volunteer forces move into the twenty-first century, each female service member is going to be watching to see if the recent changes in policy will directly affect her life. The key issues of child care, joint assignments, career progression, and sexual harassment will play a big part in retention of the female service member. For it is the dual-career couple and the active-duty female with her house husband who are out on the front lines, changing two hundred years of tradition.

★         ★         ★

# Epilogue: America's Heroines

Times have changed; time has stood still.

Sweeping changes have occurred since Uncle Sam acknowledged that his was no longer an army of single men. To accommodate the wives and families in the all-volunteer force there are now allowances for quarters, for moving household goods, and travel. Most bases are now fully equipped with chapels and movie theaters, Little League fields and bowling alleys. Counselors, psychologists, and social workers are there to smooth away the rough edges of life. The young G.I. can receive counseling on money management and budgeting. His wife has groups she can join for parenting skills. Uncle Sam nurtures all.

Yet, in looking back, there seem to be so many broken promises. Take medicine. Those who joined the service ten or twenty years ago remember vividly the promise of free medical care. It was one of the major "benefits" that made up for long hours away from home and, many times, less pay than a civilian would earn. Today, a shortage of doctors and health-care professionals has badly eroded military medicine for active-duty personnel and almost erased it for the retiree and his family. Out-of-pocket medical expenses have soared. With luck the pilot programs now being tested will alleviate these deplorable conditions and provide vitally needed continuing medical care.

In the past, the commissary and post exchange meant real savings for families. Today, any benefits they might have offered have been surpassed by civilian stores. Just another benefit eroded. Care has to be taken that the jealous "local" shopkeeper does not erode these benefits any further.

★        ★        ★

It costs—dearly—for the military family to stay with Uncle Sam. Soaring costs in the civilian sector mean each move further depletes any savings the family might have. The lower the rank of the military person, the more the hardship. There needs to be a continuing look at ways to make staying in the military economically feasible.

Emotionally, the military wife pays a high price. Even though she is not sending her husband off to war, the "cold" war is exacting a harsh toll. Some wives survive each day just a fragile fence away from the militant mobs in the Philippines or face terrorists who walk among the military in Germany. Almost every day, a military wife somewhere on the globe is burying a husband lost in a training accident or on a mission of service to his nation.

There is a different kind of courage being seen today as so many wives are doing the unheard of—defying two hundred years of tradition by speaking out about the wrongs they perceive. Witness the two wives in the work chapter who let the public know about the inequities they faced. (Now that the military has been told that the wife has a right to work, it is up to each woman to see that her basic rights are not stonewalled.) Witness the wives of the Vietnam warriors who doggedly fought for the right to know if their husbands were dead or missing in action. Witness the formation of the National Military Family Association, which has brought together women from all branches of the military and all ranks to both inform military families of their rights as well as lobby Congress for their benefits.

Each bride of Uncle Sam who completes a military career by her husband's side does so with the strong conviction that serving in the military is more than a job; it is a commitment to keep the nation strong and the gossamer threads of peace intact on this planet.

As military wives look toward the end of the century, there is tremendous cause, for pride in recent achievements and determination to work for continued progress in the future.

*              *              *

*Chapter 1*
"An Army Post," Clark, 33.
As one example, "1989 VHA rates," 37.
In trying to make ends meet, Ginvosky, "More Air Force Families," 6.
Two-thirds of its families, Givans, "Personnel Actions," 28, and Ginovsky, "Money Cuts," 14.
An E-4's allowance, *Air Force Times* Pay Chart, 34.
By 1989, *see* Pay Chart, appendix.
Says John Burlage, Burlage, "Purchasing," 3.
Author Ann Combs, Combs, 68.
Stately bricks, Gilmer, 72–75 and interviews.
Many wives have said, "Survey," 57.
Health care, Adde, "Condition Critical," 45, 48–50.
CHAMPUS, CHAMPUS Handbook, AT&T's Military Lifeguide #4, "Handbook," 34–37.
Alice Blackwell Baldwin, Baldwin, 29–31.
At Fort Leavenworth, Walton, 88.
Fort Sill, Nye, 58.
Fort Dodge, Camp Powell, Stallard, 55–57.
Falling bricks, Nye, 362, and interviews.
Col. R. Ernest Dupuy, Dupuy, 32.
In 1907, "Picking up the Tab," 67.
Wherry housing, Young, "Housing," 18, and interviews.
World-wide, Maze, "Housing costs," 18 and Young, "Housing Remains Scarce," 18.
Air Force funding, Ginovsky, "Money Cuts," 14.
Especially poor job, Maze, "Housing for Jr. Enlisted," 8, and interviews.
Overseas, Maze, "DOD: 21%", 3.

★                         ★                         ★

Minimum standards, Maze, Ibid, and Army Regulations 210–50 February 1, 1982, 7–11, 7–12.

Marine wife, Boughner, 2.

Following a nineteen-day, Maze, "Dependents," 6, *see also*, Grose, 14–18.

Release of construction money, Young, "Housing remains scarce," 18.

Services estimate, Young, Ibid.

Bellevue, "Bellevue Housing," 9.

Aliamanu Crater, Department of Army report, and interviews.

One of the latest steps, Killion, 5.

One survey noted, Blucher, "Joy," 46.

"Women's Perceived Stress," Makowsky, 111, 118.

*Chapter 2*

Martha Washington, Flexner, 14.

As Maureen Mylander, Mylander, 121.

Military manners author, Shea, 18–19.

Mylander feels, Mylander, 114.

While Shea states, Shea, 18–19.

To some extent, McCubbin, 31.

Officers' wives living on base, McCubbin, 38.

Commander's Spouse Handbook, an unpublished collection of data, differs from base to base.

A letter to the *Air Force Times*, (June 12, 1989):32.

These wives' comments, Young, A–20.

Employment an acceptable, Mylander, 121.

National League of Families, Facts Update, news releases, June 1989, and interviews.

National Military Family Association, mission goals, fact sheets, newsletters.

*Chapter 3*

"I have felt almost too wretched," Laufe, 301–302.

A survey of Navy wives, "Spouses learn man and military go hand in hand," B-6.

Noted Alice Snyder, Ph.D., material from a separate study, "Sea and Shore Rotation," 5–7.

Says Suzanne Burris, Akerlund, "Saying Goodbye," 5.

Constantine J. G. Cretekos, Cretekos, 36–37.

*Chapter 4*

No figure kept, Adde, "Surviving the unthinkable," 57, Tittle, 45, and interviews.

Time magazine review, "Revolt," 100.

★          ★          ★

The operation of the twenty houses, Allen, Riley, unpublished.
Presence of the brothels, Allen.
"For years the evil . . ." Anthony, 40.
Jay Finegan estimates, Finegan, "Sin City," 72.
Reporter P. F. Kluge, Kluge, 90.
Navy chaplain, Kluge, 163.
There seems to be a callous outlook, Maze, "Schroeder Says," 4.
As David R. Schweisberg explains, Schweisberg, A-1.
An article appearing, Ibid.
Parade magazine stated, Shearer, 8.
Military uncomfortable, Ellison, "Military Skirmishing," A-17; *see also*, Maze, "Stripes Editor," 12, 64, and Maze, "Investigative reporting," 12.
In one study, Bermudes, 218.
Excessive symptoms, Bermudes, 220.
As a result of his study, Bermudes, 223–224.
More than half, Isay, 647.
Cannot openly say, Isay, 648.
"Fact that anger," Isay, 647–648.
Documented the deterioration, Snyder, "Separation," 116–120.
5.4 more times, Snyder, Ibid, 125.
"These many problems," Snyder, Ibid, 118.
"Cessation of active sexual, Ibid, 134–135.
Snyder emphasized, 137.
"But the difference is marriage," Stone, "Sex" 129.
"Ten years as a single," Ibid, 129.
"The hardest time," Ibid, 129.

*Chapter 5*
BEHIND CLOSED DOORS, Strauss, 31.
ABUSIVE PARTNER, Roy, 9.
Researcher Strauss noted, Strauss, 3.
Six million, "Private Violence," 18.
14,382 military wives, DOD statistics, 1986, courtesy of Military Family Resource Center.
Lois A. West States, West 21–22.
Initial training, *see also*, "Law Enforcement Role," 5.
An Inspector General's report, "Service Delivery Assessment."
Young family problems, *see also* Bycer, 21, graph shows median age for adults in population at large was 40.13, for the Navy, 25.57, and for the Marines, 22.88.

★                    ★                    ★

Peter H. Neidig, Neidig, 3.
Study showed, Ibid, 4.
"There are scripts," Ibid, 4.
Study of spouse abuse, Kim, Bok Lim C., 52–53.
Researcher Murray A. Straus, Straus, 31.
"A number of difficulties," MacLennan, 7.
Typical military abuser, interviews with shelter personnel, *see also*, Bycer.
Navy Department of Medicine, interview with Lee, and Department of the Navy Instruction BUMEDINST 6320–57, Family Advocacy Programs, July 11, 1979.
Military Family Resource Center, Lee, interview.
"Armed forces rank," West, 21, and interviews.
Second-class citizens, Carrier, 28, and interviews.
"A program that works," Olander, 52.

*Chapter 6*
An article in Soldier's magazine, Miles, 49.
Nearly a quarter of a million, West, 14, Kim, Bok Lim C., 9.
Two hundred brides, interview with Chaplain Metcalf and DOD figures.
Another estimate, Kluge, 164.
Asian-American Mental Health, Kim, Sil Dong, 65, cited from West, 14.
Capt. Daniel B. Lee, Lee, "A Study."
"Women in Shadows," Kim, 53–54.
Needs assessment, Marrott, "An Assessment."
Korean woman, "Women sets self ablaze," 3, and interview.
Involvement of organized crime, Feldman, 2, *also* Anderson, C-6, and Ross, NBC transcript, 8.
One source estimates, interview with base chaplain who wishes to remain anonymous.
Even Kim, Kim, 28.
"Marriage to American," Metcalf, unpublished paper.
NBC News reporter, NBC News transcript, 8.
Nationally known columnist, Anderson, C-6.
Deputies raided five businesses, Feldman, 2.
A joint-services regulation, AR600-240 titled "Marriage in Overseas Commands."
Said one reporter, Peterson, 47.

*Chapter 7*
"Civilian attitude toward employment," Combs, 39.
Trouble in the seemingly, "Air Force Wives," AP wire copy, and Blucher, "Right to Work," 49, 52–54.

★               ★               ★

The investigation said, "Air Force Wives."

Col. Kravetz was said, "Air Force Wives."

What about the commander, "Air Force Wives."

After a subcommittee, Ginvosky, 1, 30.

Secretary of Defense, Schill, "Spouses reportedly," 10, Willis, "Ignore Marital," 8, Willis, "DOD; Marital Status," 3, 24.

Weinberger stressed, Willis, "Right to Work," 3.

The officials also emphasized, "Air Force Leaders," 3, Ginovsky, "Air Force Affirms," 1, 30, Blucher, "Right to Work," 50, 52–53, and "Air Force Leaders," 3.

Women's Equality Action League, Adams, 18.

Significant part, Becraft, 22.

"It costs the Air Force," Schroeder, "Low Morale," 26.

Unique and difficult employment, Trost, 2.

"He has his career," Stone, "Wives Who Say," 72.

Perry S. Patterson, Williams, Susanne, 46.

When the Army ran, Eisenstadt, 18.

Unemployment rate, DOD statistics, *see also* Bird, "Working," 14.

Air Force says, Bird, Ibid.

A DOD survey, Blucher, "Job of Building Career," 46.

Approximately 175,000, Gates, 110.

Civilian Personnel Officer, interviews.

"Locally hired spouses," Maze, "Full House," 6.

Five million, Korb, speech, *see also* Bird, 15.

An Air Force wife at Keesler, Blucher, "Working Solutions," 54.

It may not be working, Willis, "DOD letter," 3.

A 1987 study, Blucher, "Job of," 47.

Spouse employment centers assisted, interview with the late Pat Chong Mahaffey.

President Reagan, DOD 1404.11 passed in 1986, Blucher, "Working Solutions," 53.

*Chapter 8*

More than 223,000, Mitchell, 52, says 221,000, and "Women in the Military," 3, says female officers and enlisted figure is actually 222,338 with an addition 1,467 in the military academies to bring the total women in the military to 223,805.

As a further example, McGuire, 1–3.

9,000 women, McGuire, 2.

639 child-care centers, Maze, Rick, "Long Wait," 8, *see also*, Lorna Williams, 35, 44, 49.

Shortage of child care, Willis, "Child Care," 14.

Karen R. Keesling, Ginovsky, "A. F. Seeks," 16.

Military Family Act, pamphlet, "Operating Home-Based Business in Military Housing," Military Family Resource Center.

DOD issued new guidelines, Johnson, 1, *see also*, Schill, "DOD issues," 15.

Child care is costly, Ginovsky, "AF Seeks," 16, Maze, "Minding the Kids," 14 and Maze, "Long Waits," 8.

Children's safety, Maze, "Some child care," 8, 34–35.

Closed and demolished, "Army to Close," 2.

Three pre-schoolers, Budahn, "3 at Army," 4.

Two parents filed suit, Givans, "Successful Appeal," 8, and Maze, "Parents Fear," 6, 69.

Separate incident, Maze, "Dismissed," 10.

Reporter David W. Givans, Givans, "Successful appeal," 8.

Academy graduate explained, Adde, "Married and in Uniform," 53, 58–59.

That same sentiment, Adde, "At the Crossroads," 81, Adde, "The First Female," 81.

In fact, "Spouse Issue Blue Ribbon," 14.

Army specialist, Borgnino, "G. I. Mom," A-10.

A woman naval captain, Longo, 10.

Opened 200 support, Willis, "DOD Opens," 1.

David J. Armor, Ibid, 3.

Rep. Beverly B. Byron, Willis, "Expanded role," 3.

Sexual harassment, Halloran, "Advisers Say," 5, "Naval Officer Charged," 3, and "Military Sexual Harassment," 2.

A study by, "Military Sexual Harassment," 2.

Rep. Schroeder, Willis, "Expanded role," 3.

★                    ★                    ★

COLA or cost-of-living allowance is a variable amount determined by the cost of living. It varies from location to location.

COMP TIME is compensation. The military is not a nine-to-five job. There is no overtime pay. When service members take time off for personal business during work hours, it's called comp time.

DUTY, as in "standing the duty," is a military term for being at the ready. It is a special detail. Duty schedules can vary. "One in three" in which the person stands the duty one day out of three, is one example. The schedule depends on the seniority of the military member, the outfit, and the mission to which the military member is assigned.

FAMILY SERVICE CENTERS were created to serve the families of the All Volunteer Service. While each center differs as to size and personnel, most offer counseling and referrals in all family matters. Classes often held include: financial planning, surviving while spouses are gone, parenting, and programs for foreign-born wives. Other special-interest classes are also offered.

FLOATS is a marine term to designate a training period, including at-sea time.

HOUSING ALLOWANCE. Each pay grade is alloted a housing allowance. If the military member lives in base housing, that amount is deducted from his/her pay as "rent." When living off base it is added to the take home pay.

OMBUDSMAN PROGRAM is a Navy program that trains people to act as liaisons between the Navy and the family. The ombudsman receives training to enable him or her to spot potential problems and get the person in touch with a care-giver.

REMOTE is an assignment without the family, usually no less than one year.

★                                    ★                                    ★

TDY or temporary additional duty can run from days to weeks to months. The service member goes TDY without the family.

VHA or Variable Housing Allowance is an amount added to the housing allowance to compensate for high cost of living areas (see chart).

WARDROOM is a Navy/Coast Guard term for that part of the ship/boat reserved for officers. It includes sleeping quarters as well as dining quarters and is off limits to enlisted.

★        ★        ★

# Bibliography

*Books and Magazine Articles*

Adde, Nick. "Condition Critical." *Life in the Times*, (August 8, 1985): 45, 48–50.

———. "At the Crossroads: First female academy graduate now making career decisions." Ibid., (May 19, 1986): 81.

———. "Married and in Uniform." Ibid., (July 25, 1988): 53, 58–59.

———. "The Navy vs. Colts Neck." Ibid., (June 8, 1987): 49, 52–54.

———. "Surviving the Unthinkable—Infidelity." Ibid. (Feb. 24, 1986): 57, 66–67.

Akerlund, Dr. Kathy. "Saying Goodbye, It Hurts to See Your Whole Life on a Moving Van." *Life in the Times*, (February 6, 1984): 5.

Alvarez, A. "A Reporter at Large, Offshore—1." *New Yorker*, (January 20, 1986): 34–36, 39–50, 52–70.

Anthony, J. Garner. *Hawaii Under Army Rule*. Honolulu: University of Hawaii Press, 1955.

"Assignment: Japan." *The Times Magazine*, (August 5, 1985): 1–21.

Baldwin, Alice Blackwell. *An Army Wife on the Frontier*. Salt Lake City, Utah: University of Utah, 1975.

Basic Pay, Housing graphs, *Air Force Magazine*, (May 1987): 83–84.

Beck, Dee. "We Can Make Life Easier for Foreign-born Wives." *Times Magazine*, (August 7, 1978): 48–58.

———. "Will She Be Happy in the States." *Off Duty*, Pacific (October 1984): 1.

Becraft, Carolyn Howland. "Role Conflict and the Commander's Spouse: A Personal Reflection." *Military Chaplains' Review*, (Winter 1988): 21–28.

Bermudes, Robert W. "A Ministry to the Repeatedly Grief-Stricken." *Journal of Pastoral Care*, Vol. 27 (4) (1973): 218–228.

Bernath, Clifford, Maj. *Making the Most of It*. Harrisburg, Pennsylvania: Stackpole Books, 1983.

Blucher, Jay. "The Job of Building a Career." *Life in the Times*, (February 16, 1987): 46.

———. "The Right to Work." Ibid., (August 3, 1987): 50, 52–53.

———. "Working Solutions." Ibid., (February 23, 1987): 53.

Boswell, Susan M. "The Good Navy Wife." *Redbook*, (August 1975): 116, 118–120.

Boughner, Debra L. "But in Okinawa," Letter to editor. *The Times Magazine*, (October 7, 1985): 2

Branden, Nathaniel. "How to Raise Your Self-Esteem." *New Woman*, (May 1987): 41–43.

Brown, Judith. "Home Business: A Perfect Option for Military Wives." *Family*, (March 1986).

Clark, Maureen. *Captain's Bride, General's Lady*. New York: McGraw-Hill, 1956.

Clute, Sara Anne Vander. "Whither Thou Goest . . . Sometimes." *Life in the Times*, (February 7, 1983): 15–16.

Combs, Ann. *Smith College Never Taught Me How to Salute*. New York: Harper & Row, 1981.

Conroy, Pat. *The Great Santini*. Boston: Houghton Mifflin Company, 1976.

Cragg, Dan, Sgt. Maj. USA Ret. *The Guide to Military Installations*. Harrisburg, Pennsylvania: Stackpole Books, 1983.

Cretekos, Constantine J. G., M.D. "Common Psychological Syndromes of the Army Wife." *Military Medicine*, (138(1) 1973): 36–37.

Distelheim, Rochelle. "There's a Time Bomb Ticking Inside Me." *Family Circle*, (October 1985): 46, 48, 80, 82.

Dobach, R. Emerson, Russell Dobach. *Violence Against Wives*. New York: The Free Press, 1979.

Dupuy, Col. R. Ernest. *The Compact History of the United States Army*. New York: Hawthorn Books, Inc., 1956.

———. "Pass in Review." *The Army Combat Forces Journal*, (October 1954): 32.

"Feminism May Threaten Factors Used to Control Military Wives." *U.S. Medicine*, (October 1976): 2, 7.

Finegan, Jay. "Service Marriages." *Life in the Times*, (February 7, 1983): 4, 6, 8–9.

———. "Sin City." Ibid., (April 28, 1986): 65, 72–73.

Flexner, Eleanor. *Century of Struggle*. New York: Atheneum, 1973.

★        ★        ★

Gabower, Genevieve, D.S.W. "Behavior Problems of Children in Navy Officers' Families." *Social Casework*, 4(4): 177–184.

Ganoe, William Addleman. *The History of the United States Army*, revised ed. New York: D. Appleton-Century Company, 1942.

Gates, Ed. "Working Wives—Few Opportunities Overseas." *Air Force Magazine*, (February 1981): 111.

Gibbons, Sheila. "Commanders' Wives." *LadyCom*, (June 1984): 51–57, 63–65, 70

Gilmer, La Jeanne T. "At Home in the Bricks." *Military Lifestyle*, (October 1988): 72–75.

Godwin, Carol. "It Takes a Lot of Love." Ibid., (October 1986): 18–19, 22, 55.

Goldman, Nancy L., and David R. Segal, eds. *The Social Psychology of Military Service*. Beverly Hills: Sage Publications, 1976.

Griffith, Robert K., Jr. *Men Wanted for the U.S. Army*. Westport, Connecticut: Greenwood Press, 1982.

Gritz, Gloria. "The Changing Commander's Wife." *Life in the Times*, (August 11, 1986): 57, 64–65.

Gross, Mary Preston. *Mrs. NCO*. Chuluota, Florida: Beau Lac Publishers, 1969.

"Handbook for Military Families." *The Times Magazine*, (April 1, 1985).

Hartog, Joseph, M.D "Group Therapy with Psychotic and Borderline Military Wives." *American Journal of Psychiatry*, (April 1966): 122: 1125–1131.

Hill, Reuben. *Families Under Stress*. Westport, Connecticut: Greenwood Press, 1949.

"Housing." *The Times Magazine*, (April 1, 1985): 63, 64, 66–67.

"Housing, Expensive Off Base, Scarce On Base." *The Times Magazine*, (June 6, 1983): 10–11, 14.

Hunter, Edna J. *Families Under the Flag, A Review of Military Family Literature*. New York: Praeger, 1982.

Hunter, Edna J., and D. Stephen Nice, eds. *Military Families, Adaption to Change*. New York: Praeger Publishers, 1978.

Isay, Richard A. "The Submariners' Wives Syndrome." *Psychiatric Quarterly*, 42(4) (October 1968): 647–652.

Janowitz, Morris. *The Professional Soldier*. Morris Janowitz, The Free Press of Glencoe, 1961.

Kaslow, Florence W., and Richard I. Ridenour. *The Military Family*. New York: The Guilford Press, 1984.

Kavanaugh, Mildred. "Coffees, Teas, But Without Me." *LadyCom*, (1973).

Kim, Bok-Lim C., M.S.W. *Women in Shadows*. National Committee Concerned with Asian Wives of U.S. Servicemen. La Jolla, California: 1981.

King, Edward L. *The Death of the Army*. New York: The Saturday Review Press, 1972.

Kinzer, Betty and Marion Leach. *What Every Army Wife Should Know*. Harrisburg, Pennsylvania: Stackpole Books, 1966.

Kluge, P. F. "Why They Love Us in the Philippines." *Playboy*, (September 1986): 89–90, 162–164.

Knight, Oliver. *Life and Manners in the Frontier Army*. Norman, Oklahoma: University of Oklahoma Press, 1978.

Kozaryn, Linda. "Sole Parent Soldiers." *Family*, (February 1981): 23–26, 28.

Krider, Scott. "The Mrs. Wears a Mustache." *LadyCom*, (September 1985).

LeGrove. D. M. "The Military Family Syndrome." *American Journal of Psychiatry*, (1978) 135: 1040–1043.

Levitan, Sar A., and Karen Cleary Alderman. *Warriors at Work*. The Volunteer Armed Forces. Beverly Hills, California: Sage Publications, 1977.

"Liberation Movement Seen Detrimental to Marriage." *U.S. Medicine*, (October 1, 1976): 2, 6.

*Listen, the War*. Colorado: USAF Academy Associate of Graduates, 1973.

Little, Roger, ed. *Handbook of Military Institutions*. Beverly Hills: Sage, 1971.

"Looking from the Inside Out." *Time*, (October 3, 1977): 85.

MacIntosh, Houston, M.D. "Separation Problems in Military Wives." *American Journal of Psychiatry*, (August 1968): 125:2, 260–265.

Madden, Linda K. "When Promotion Comes: How Should a Wife React?" *The Times Magazine*, (June 3, 1985).

Margiotta, Franklin D., ed. *The Changing World of the American Military*. Boulder, Colorado: Westview Press, 1978.

Martin, D. *Battered Wives*. New York: Simon and Schuster, 1976.

Matloff, Maurice, ed. *American Military History*. Washington, D.C.: Office of the Chief of Military History, U.S. Army, 1969.

McCall, Celeste. "The Homecoming." *The Times Magazine*, (March 2, 1981): 5–7.

McCorkle, Emily Fitzgerald; Laufe, Abe, ed. *An Army Doctor's Wife on the Frontier*. Pittsburgh, Pennsylvania: University of Pittsburgh Press, 1962.

McCubbin, Hamilton I., Barbara B. Dahl, and Edna J. Hunter, eds. *Families in the Military System*. Beverly Hills: Sage Publications, 1976.

McCubbin, Hamilton I., and Martha A. Marsden; Margiotta, Franklin D. ed. "The Military Family and the Changing Military Profession." *The*

*Changing World of the American Military*. Boulder, Colorado: Westview Press, 1978.

Miles, Donna. "Bicultural Marriage." *Soldiers*, (June 1989).

"Military Family Programs: New Rationale, New Approaches." *American Family*, (Vol. IV, No. 5): 6.

Minton, Eric. "Don't Call Me Dependent." *The Times Magazine*, (September 2, 1985).

Mitchell, Brian. "Women Don't Belong in the Military." *Life in the Times*, (July 3, 1989): 45, 52–53.

"Monthy Basic Allowance for Quarters." *Air Force Magazine*, (May 1987): 83.

Morgan, Maj. R. P. "The Married Soldier—Problems and Ponderings." *Army Quarterly*, (October 1966).

Mosley, Leonard. *Hero for Our Times*. New York: Hearst Books, 1982.

Murphy, Mary Kay and Carol Bowles Parker. *Fitting in as a New Service Wife*. Harrisburg, Pennsylvania: Stackpole Press, 1966.

Mylander, Maureen. *The Generals*. New York: Dial Press, 1974.

Nichols, Claudia. "Can You Really Ruin Your Husband's Career?" *Life in the Times*, (September 29, 1986).

———. "If Your Husband Beats You." *Air Force Times* magazine supplement, (January 12, 1981): 4–8.

———. "Real Moving Stories." *Life in the Times* (special issue on moving), (February 6, 1984): 33.

Nye, W. S. *Carbine and Lance: The Story of Old Fort Sill*. Norman, Oklahoma: University of Oklahoma Press. 1937.

O'Beirne, Kathleen P. "Pits & Palaces, Military Housing Status Report." *Family*, (August 1983): 22–28.

Olander, Cmdr. E. A., CHC, USN. "AMENDS, Abusive men exploring new directions." *Military Chaplains Review*, Vol. 15, No. 2 (Spring 1986): 43–52.

Owens-Graves, C. "If He's At Sea, You Don't Have to Be." *Life in the Times*, (January 27, 1986): 71.

Pearlman, Chester A. "Separation Reactions of Married Women." American Journal of Psychiatry, 126(7) (January 1970): 946–950.

Peterson, MSGT. Mary. "Tying the Knot Overseas." *Soldiers*, (June 1989): 47.

"Picking up the Tab for Housing: Evolution of the BAQ System." *Life in the Times*, (April 1, 1985): 67.

Poniske, John D., and Linda G. Jensen. "When the Husband Is the 'Dependent.' " Ibid., (February 7, 1983): 22, 26, 28.

★      ★      ★

"Private Violence." *Time*, (September 5, 1983): 18–19.

"Revolt of Mamie Stover." *Time*, (May 28, 1956): 67.

Riley, Rene. "Military Wives in Revolt." *U.S. News and World Report*, (April 18, 1988): 38.

Robinson, Sue. "I Do. Really Do." *LadyCom*, (March 1984): 48–51.

Roy, Maria. ed. *The Abusive Partner*. New York: Van Nostrand Publications, 1982.

Satchell, Michael, et al. "The Military's New Stars." *U.S. News and World Report*, (April 18, 1988): 32–40.

Schwabe, Mario R., and Florence W. Kaslow; Kaslow, Florence W., and Ridenour, Richard I., eds. "Violence in the Military Family." *Military Family*. New York: The Guilford Press, 1984.

Shea, Nancy. *The Air Force Wife*. New York: Harper and Row, 1966.

Shearer, Lloyd. "Sex Scandal Brewing." *Parade*, (August 3, 1986): 8.

Slavin, Peter. "AIDS Comes Home." *Life in the Times*, (March 23, 1987): 41, 44.

———. "The AIDS Threat." Ibid., (March 30, 1987): 41, 43–45.

———. "Our Terrible Fate." Ibid., (August 31, 1987): 65, 68–69.

———. "Young and Struggling." Ibid., (April 18, 1988): 57, 62–63.

Snowcroft, LG Brent. *Military Service in the United States*. Englewood Cliffs, N.J.: Prentice Hall, Inc., 1982.

"Sole Parents." *Commanders Call*, (March–April 1979): 2–5.

Stallard, Patricia Y. *Glittering Misery*. San Rafael, California: Presidio Press and Fort Collins, Colorado: The Old Army Press, 1978.

Steinmetz, Suzanne K. *The Cycle of Violence*. New York: Praeger, 1977.

Stone, Bonnie Domrose. "Sex and Separations." *LadyCom*, (October 1976): 27–29.

———. "Sex and Separations: Some Candid Interviews with Military Couples." Ibid. 45–46.

———. "The Time Alone." *Marriage and Family Living*, 56(8): (August 1974) 2–4.

———. "The Time Alone: How to Cope When the Man of the House Isn't There." *Honolulu*, (July 1986): 48–49, 69–71.

———. "Wives Who Say: I Won't." *LadyCom*, (June/July 1983): 70, 72–74.

Straus, Murray A., Richard J. Gelles, Suzanne K. Steinmetz. *Behind Closed Doors, Violence in the American Family*. New York: Doubleday, Anchor Books, 1980.

"Survey." *Life in the Times*, (March 20, 1989): 57.

★                              ★                              ★

Tittle, Bess M. "Infidelity & Need." *LadyCom*, (April 1985): 45–47, 58, 60–62.

Vandervelde, Maryanne. *The Changing Life of the Corporate Wife*. New York: Mecox Publishing Co., 1979.

Waldo, Michael. "Group Counseling for Military Personnel Who Batter Their Wives." *Journal for Specialists in Group Work*, (September 1986): 132–138.

Walton, George. *Sentinel of the Plains*. Fort Leavenworth and the American West. Englewood Cliffs, New Jersey: Prentice-Hall, Inc., 1973.

Weissman, Myrna. "The Depressed Woman: Recent Research." *Social Work*, 17(5): 24, 1972.

Wendt, Jo Ann. "The Other Kinds of Infidelity." *Life in the Times*, (February 7, 1983): 30, 32.

West, Lois A., William M. Turner, Ellen Dunwoody. *Wife Abuse in the Armed Forces*. Washington, D.C.: Center for Women Policy Studies, 1981.

"Where Should Military Families Live?" *Family*, (June 1987).

Williams, Lorna. "Desperately Seeking Daycare." *Military Lifestyle*, (October 1988): 36–39.

Williams, Susanne. "Military Wives and the Job Chase." *LadyCom*, (April 1984): 46.

Young, Nancy. "Choices." *Off Duty*, (August 1986).

*Newspapers*

"1989 VHA Rates." *Air Force Times*, (January 9, 1989): 37.

Adams, Roy. "Wives reportedly still pressured to quit jobs." Ibid. (January 2, 1988): 18.

Adde, Nick. "The Day the Earth Stood Still." Ibid., (February 20, 1989): 46, 52–54.

"Air Force Leaders State Policy on Working Wives." Ibid., (August 10, 1987): 3.

"Air Force Times Pay Chart." Ibid., (January 2, 1989): 34.

"Air Force Wives." Associated Press, Washington, D.C.: (October 9, 1987).

Anderson, Jack and Dale van Atta. " 'Military Procurement' means hookers for troops in Korea." *Antelope Valley Press*, (August 13, 1989): C-6.

Armstrong, Jay A. "Base Commander's Views on Abuse Case Disputed." *Air Force Times*, (September 19, 1988): 22.

"Army to close center amid sex abuse charges." *Pacific Stars and Stripes*. (November 17, 1987): 2.

★               ★               ★

Bird, Julie. "Working Spouses." Ibid., (May 15, 1989): 14, 15, 18.

Blucher, Jay. "Your Turn: Should Senior Wives Work?" *Air Force Times*, (August 24, 1987).

"Blue Ribbon Panel Files Spouse Finding." *The Kadena Shogun*, (January 15, 1988).

Boersema, Staff Sergeant James M. "Over Here and (Sometimes) Overwhelmed." *SAM*, (August 1980).

Bognino, Charles M. "GI Mom Gets Wish—to Be a Civilian." *Times Herald*, (March 22, 1989): A-10.

Boorda, Vice Admiral Mike. "The Navy's Primary Commitment Must Be to Its People." *Navy Times*, (March 20, 1989).

Budahn, P. J. "Members With Kin Hurt Most by PCS Weight Limits." *Air Force Times*, (May 25, 1988): 3.

———. "3 at Army Child Care Center has V.D." Ibid., (August 24, 1987): 4.

Burgess, Tom. "Frequent Short Absences Take Toll on Children." *Navy Times*, (September 9, 1985): 3.

Burlage, John. "Housing costs often influence career decision." *Air Force Times*, (July 4, 1988): 1, 18, 32.

———. "New Rule Eases Overseas Low-Cost Moves." Ibid., (May 23, 1988): 3.

———. "Purchasing power of military pay up slightly." Ibid., (February 13, 1989): 3, 69.

———. "Push on for Higher VHA: Survey in March." *Navy Times*, (February 22, 1988): 1, 34.

———. "Ruling Denies ex-wife share of retired pay." *Air Force Times*, (January 16, 1989): 17.

———. "Statistics Hint Military Career Appeal Is Fading." Ibid., (October 17, 1988): 4.

Carrier, Allen E. "Spouse Perception: 'Second-Class Citizens.' " *Army Times*, (January 10, 1983): 28.

"Child care shortage could last five years or more." *Air Force Times*, (April 18, 1988): 14.

Clark, Carol. "She Seeks Better Life for Military Families." Oahu, Hawaii, *Central/Military Sun Press*, (January 9–15, 1986): B-2.

Dalton, Pat. "Job Programs for Spouses to Begin at Family Centers." *Air Force Times*, (February 15, 1988): 3, 24.

"Demands on Wives a Disgrace." *Air Force Times*, (August 31, 1987).

"DOD Letter Stresses Spouses' Right to Work." Ibid., (November 2, 1987).

\*  \*  \*

"DOD Survey Leads to Better Family Programs." Ibid., (August 10, 1987).

Eisenstadt, Steven. "Army Spouses Grumble over Family Programs." *Army Times*, (November 30, 1987): 1, 18.

Ellison, Katherine. "Military is skirmishing on its own news front." Honolulu *Star-Bulletin*, Ibid., (September 28, 1986): A-17.

"Family day care has advantages: questions, answers for parents." *Desert Wings*, (February 19, 1988): 9.

Faulhaber, Linda. "Child-care center feels the squeeze." *Antelope Valley Press*, (November 17, 1988): A3–A4.

———. "Edwards AFB personnel face housing crunch." Ibid., (November 11, 1988): A4.

———. "Korean spouses find culture-shock support." Ibid., (November 8, 1988): B7.

———. "Young enlisted personnel often left out in cold." Ibid., (November 11, 1988): A5.

Feldman, Paul. "Five Sites Raided in Move to Sever Alleged String of Korean Brothels." *Los Angeles Times*, (August 7, 1988): 2.

Ferry, Marie E. "DOD: Survey Leads to Better Family Programs." *Air Force Times*, (August 10, 1987): 6.

Foglesong, Colonel Robert H. "AF Mapping a Long Term Strategy to Improve Retention of Pilots." *Air Force Times*, (June 19, 1989): 24–25.

Fritsch, Jane. "They're looking for a few good men, with sensitivity to train marines." Ibid., (January 3, 1989): 22.

Garamone, Jim. "Officers' Wives Dispute Club's Disbandment." *Air Force Times*, (February 17, 1986): 3.

Ginovsky, John. "AF Affirms Spouse Right to Hold Job." *Air Force Times*, (March 28, 1988): 1, 30.

———. "AF Fears Further Loss of Mechanics to Airlines." Ibid., (March 20, 1989): 3.

———. "AF Seeks expanded child care services." Ibid., (April 24, 1989): 16.

———. "Air Force Trying to Change Conditions that Push Pilots Out." Ibid., (January 16, 1989): 11.

———. "Binnicker Tells Hill Better Housing Is Key to Retention." Ibid., (March 13, 1989): 3.

———. "Money Cuts Slow Family Housing Renovation." Ibid., (May 23, 1988): 14.

———. "More AF Families Use Food Stamps at Commissaries." Ibid., (August 14, 1989): 6.

——. "Pease AFB to Test Unique Renovation Plan." Ibid., (June 27, 1988): 7.

——. "Wife of Only Listed POW Believes He Is Alive." Ibid., (May 12, 1986): 10.

——. "Wives pressured to quit working, inquiry finds." Ibid., (October 26, 1987): 4.

Givans, David W. "Money Cuts Slow Family Housing Renovation." *Air Force Times*, (May 23, 1988): 14.

——. "Personnel Actions Affect Wait for Base Quarters." Ibid., (May 2, 1988): 3.

——. "Plan for Self-Supporting Clubs Called 'Devastating.' " Ibid., (May 9, 1988): 8.

——. "Successful Appeal Furthers Scott Day Care Lawsuit." Ibid., (February 15, 1988): 8.

Grant, Willis. "Child Care Shortage Could Last 5 Years or More." *Air Force Times*, (April 8, 1988).

Grose, Thomas. "Naples duty registers high on Richter scale." *Navy Times*, (June 19, 1989): 14–18.

Halloran, Richard. "Advisers say servicewomen abused." Los Angeles *Daily News*, (September 17, 1987): 5.

"Hanky-panky Is Strictly Off Limits." *Insight/Washington Times*, (February 15, 1988): 11: E3-E-5.

Harris, Evelyn Doyle. "Service rule on home-based businesses discussed." American Forces Information Service, *Desert Wings*, (December 9, 1988): 3.

"Job Breaks for Dependent Wives Urged." *Stars & Stripes*, (November 21, 1981).

Johnson, Julie. "Military Facing Child Care Crisis." *Daily Press*, (June 25, 1989): 1.

Killion, Cindy. "Outreach fights family isolation." *Mountaineer*, (July 14, 1989): 5.

Landers, Ann. "Navy wife finds her life at home is unbearable." *Daily News*, (September 25, 1987): 5.

Longo, James. "Navy Taps Byerly as Women's Policy Chief." *Navy Times*, (February 22, 1988): 10.

Maze, Rick. "Dependents overseas reassessed." *Air Force Times*, (January 2, 1989): 6, 61.

——. "Dismissed sex-abuse case angers Army parents." Ibid., (August 29, 1988): 10.

————. DOD: 21% of Families Lack Acceptable Housing." Ibid., (December 29, 1986): 3.

————. "DOD: Half of Off-Base Junior EM Housing Poor." Ibid., (January 5, 1987): 3.

————. "4% Pay Raise Advances Through Committee." Ibid., (April 11, 1988): 4.

————. "Full House Defeats Measure Limiting Spouse Teaching Jobs." Ibid., (May 23, 1988): 6.

————. "Housing for Junior Enlisteds 'Needs Attention.' " Ibid., (December 8, 1986): 8, 20, 47.

————. "Housing Problems Persist Despite Improvements." Ibid., (December 22, 1986): 7.

————. "Investigative reporting ban backed by DOD." Ibid., (January 9, 1989): 12, 64.

————. "Jan. 1 Increases Set, Pay 4.1 Percent, BAQ 7 Percent." Ibid., (July 4, 1988): 1, 31.

————. "Long Waits, Lower Fees for Military Daycare." Ibid., (September 14, 1987): 8.

————. "Military Handling of Child Abuse Comes Under Increased Scrutiny." Ibid., (May 2, 1988): 29.

————. "Minding the kids, legislation would improve, widen military child care." Ibid., (April 3, 1989): 14.

————. "Parents fear cover-ups of day-care abuse." Ibid., (August 22, 1988): 6, 69.

————. "Schroeder Says AF Best in Far East Family Care." Ibid., (September 15, 1986): 4.

————. "Some Child Centers Too Old, Pose Risks." Ibid., (September 14, 1987): 8, 34–35.

————. "Stripes editor defends his news judgment." Ibid., (January 9, 1989): 12, 64.

————. "Study Links Family Attitude to Retention." Ibid., (May 14, 1984).

"Military Child Care." Ibid., (September 14, 1987).

"Military Sexual Harassment, A Study: Women in Pacific Hardest Hit." *Pacific Stars and Stripes*, (September 19, 1987): 2.

"Military Still Pay More for Moves Than Civilians." Ibid., (May 16, 1988): 10.

Moore, Molly. "Parents in the Military Find Hardship in Leave Policies." *Los Angeles Times*, (May 15, 1988): 2, 36.

"More Married Members Strain Other Services." *Air Force Times*, (November 17, 1986).

Morse, Harold. "Navy Official Has High Praise for Pacific Command Families." *Honolulu Star-Bulletin*, (February 12, 1986): A-14.

———. "19,000 Military Homes on Oahu Amount to a City Unto Themselves." Ibid., (June 23, 1986): A-1-3.

———. "66,709 Military Dependents Here." Ibid., (April 13, 1983): A-1, A-12.

"Navy Officer Charged with Sexual Harassment." (United Press International) *Pacific Stars and Stripes*, (September 21, 1987): 3.

"Portrait of Military Shows Surprise." *Pueblo Chieftain*, (September 28, 1986).

"Pulling alert duty." *Air Force Times*, (September 12, 1988): 27.

Rangel, Enrique. "Men turning to Philippines in search of wives." *Daily News*, (July 8, 1989): 3.

Reed, Fred. "Military defines 'free press' differently from civilians." Ibid., (April 24, 1988): 4.

Riddle, Lyn. "Military Life a Roadblock to Adoption." *New York Times*, (March 26, 1989): 18.

Robinson, Brigadier General Peter G. "Spouses Vital to National Defense Readiness." *The Kadena Shogun*, (May 13, 1988).

Roland, Neil. "Despite Deaths, Care at Madigan Found Good." *Army Times*, (July 1, 1985): 1.

Schill, Charlie. "Spouses reportedly still pressured to quit jobs." *Air Force Times*, (December 5, 1988): 10.

———. "Child-care funding inadequate, Carlucci warns." Ibid., (February 13, 1989): 19.

———. DOD Issues New Guidelines to Standardize Child Care." Ibid., (April 3, 1989): 15.

Schroeder, Patricia. "Low Morale Threatens Military Readiness." Ibid., (April 27, 1987): 26.

"Schroeder Says Far East Best in Family Care." Ibid., (September 15, 1986).

Schweisberg, David R. "Weak dollar puts women in bar jobs." *Pacific Stars and Stripes*, (May 27, 1986): A-1.

Shoemaker, Randall. "New Basic Pay Rates Change Benefit Picture." *Air Force Times*, (February 8, 1988): 18.

" 'Single Parent' must bear the responsibility of Two." Norfolk *Virginian-Pilot*, (February 7, 1988): 11: B3, B4, B5.

Slavin, Peter. "So You Want to Adopt." *Air Force Times*, (February 13, 1989): 47, 52–53.

★               ★               ★

Smith, Maj. Pete. "Army Life's Problems." *Army* (Australia), (March 20, 1986): 1.

"Spouses Have Right to Work," *Air Force Times*. (January 25, 1988).

"Spouses learn man and military go hand in hand." Norfolk *Virginian-Pilot*, (February 7, 1988): B6—8.

Stone, Bonnie. "Parenting Solo." *Army Times*, (November 1, 1982): 51.

"Study: Working, Happy Wives Fared Better in Long Separation." *Air Force Times*, (May 10, 1988): 10, 26.

"Style of Military Life Said Critical to EM Retention." Ibid., (May 12, 1986).

Townsend, Staff Sergeant Carole J. "Male Dependent." *Army Times* (letter to the editor), (April 11, 1983): 24.

"We are Not a Male-Order Bride Service." *Pacific Stars and Stripes*, (March 3, 1986).

"Weinberger Sets Policy: Military Wives Have Right to Work." Ibid., (October 26, 1987): 3.

Williams, Sgt. Maj. Rudi. "DOD reports deaths resulting from child and spouse abuse." *Desert Wings* California (November 13, 1987): 1.

Willis, Grant, "CHAMPUS Test may end because of contractor's woes." *Navy Times*, (June 19, 1989): 8, 18.

———. "Child Care Shortage Could Last Five Years or More." *Air Force Times*, (April 18, 1988): 14.

———. "DOD Letter Stresses Spouse's Right to Work." Ibid., (November 2, 1987): 3.

———. "DOD Opens 2,000 Jobs in Aircrews to AF Women." Ibid., (February 15, 1988): 1, 3.

———. "DOD: Marital Status Irrelevant in Most Personnel Decisions." Ibid., (February 15, 1988): 3, 24.

———. "Expanded Role for Military Women Described as 'Important First Step.' " Ibid., (February 15, 1988): 3.

———. "Ignore Marital Stats, Carlucci Orders Board." Ibid., (January 25, 1988): 8.

———. "Member's Wife Said to Be Spreading AIDS." Ibid., (July 27, 1987): 16.

———. "Some CHAMPUS users decry billing problems." Ibid., (May 8, 1989): 6

———. "Study Links Officer Retention, Spouse Jobs." Ibid., (April 18, 1988): 14.

———. "The other CHAMPUS." Ibid., (February 6, 1989): 14–16.

———. "Wives Pressured to Quit Work Inquiry Finds." Ibid., (January 25, 1988): 8.

"Woman Sets Self Ablaze." *Honolulu Advertiser*, (November 5, 1974): 3.

"Working wives of military men tell of threats." (Associated Press Wire Service) *Antelope Valley Press*, (October 11, 1987): C4.

Young, Sharon B. "Housing Remains Scarce Despite Construction." *Air Force Times*, (October 6, 1986): 18.

———. "Military Allows Stable Family Life, Panel Says." Ibid., (September 8, 1986): 17.

*Government Documents/Publications/Surveys/Studies*

Aliamanu Family Life Center, Hawaii, activities program.

Aliamanu Military Reservation Community Mediation Service, Information Paper.

Allen, Riley. "The Fight on Tolerated Prostitution Has Just Begun." Honolulu: unpublished paper. Presented at the Social Protection Meeting of the Honolulu Council of Social Agencies, on Social Hygiene Day, (February 7, 1945). (University of Hawaii, Hamilton Library, Hawaiian/Pacific Room.)

American Academy of Family Physicians brochure.

American Women's Activities, History. (Germany).

"Area-Building Leader Responsibilities." Department of the Air Force. Kaiserslautern Military Community directive. (September 8, 1983).

Army Family of Two Million Plus Served by Effective Network of Support Systems. Status report (undated) by *Military Family*.

Army Family, White Paper (1983), Chief of Staff, United States Army.

AT&T Military Lifeguide, #4, CHAMPUS.

Attitude Survey of Civilian Housing Residents, Hawaii (1986).

"Bellevue Housing Area and USO Work to Bring Community Together." *Military Family*, (September/October 1982): 9.

Boles, Brigadier General Billy J., USAF, Division of Personnel Programs. "Retention and Readiness Tied to Family Support." *Air Force Family Matters*, (December 1987): 1, 3–4.

Bycer, Alene M., John D. Fluke, Theresa C. Allen, Patricia Schene, Linda B. Suski. *Navy Family Advocacy Program*. Denver, Colorado. Children's Division: The American Humane Society (June 1984). (Organizational Effectiveness Research Program, Office of Naval Research)

"CHAMPUS Handbook," Aurora, Colorado.

★              ★              ★

"Commanders' Wives' Handbook," unpublished, differs from base to base.

Department of the Army, Draft Environmental Statement, Military Family Housing Project, Aliamanu Military Reservation, Oahu, Hawaii (December 1974).

Department of Defense Child Abuse and Neglect Statistical Report.

Department of Defense "Family Advocacy Program," (July 10, 1986).

Department of Defense Spouse Abuse Statistics for Fiscal Year 1983, 1984, 1985, 1986.

Department of Defense Spouse Preference Program, handout.

Erickson, Major Bonee, ed. *The Other Half, A Practical Survival Guide for the Air Force Officer's Spouse*, Air Command and Staff College, Class of 1983.

Equal Opportunity, #1585 (May 27, 1987).

Equal Opportunity, #1543 (February 10, 1987).

"Facts About the Specialty of Family Practice," AAFP Reprint 304, 2: 1981.

*Families in Blue*, Chief of Chaplains for the Air Force (1980, 1986).

"Family Doctors Focus on Care, Prevention," The American Academy of Family Physicians.

"Family Resources," *Military Family*.

Family Service Center Program, Department of the Navy, OPNAV Instruction 1754.1A (August 8, 1985).

Family Support Center Calendar of Events, Edwards AFB, California.

Family Support Program Briefing, Department of the Navy, Pearl Harbor, Hawaii.

"Five Types of Abuse," Military Spouse Abuse Shelter, Honolulu, Hawaii.

Ganley, Anne L., Ph.D. "Court-Mandated Counseling for Men who Batter: A Three-Day Workshop for Mental Health Professionals. Participants Manual." Washington, D.C.: Center for Women Policy Studies.

Griffith, Janet D., Lisa M. LaVange, Tim J. Gabel. "Description of Spouses of Officers and Enlisted Personnel in the U.S. Armed Forces: 1985. Research Triangle Institute and Defense Manpower Data Center." (November 1986.) Vol. 1.

"Guidelines for recognizing spouse abuse," Military Family Resource Center, (1989): 1–25.

"Handbook for Military Families." *Times*, 1985 Edition.

"Herstory—Women's Advocacy History." Germany.

Hickam AFB Family Support Center Folder.

Hunter, Edna J. and Thomas C. Shaylor. *The Military Family and the Military Organization*. Washington, D.C.: The Adjutant General Center, (1978).

"Information for Our Patients," Army Handout, Tripler Army Medical Center, Hawaii.

Kim, Bok-Lim C. and Betty Bassoff. Draft of "A Manual for Service Providers Working with Bi-cultural Military Families."

Kim, Sil Dong, "An Analysis of Problems of Asian Wives of U.S. Servicemen," Seattle: Demonstration Project for Asian Americans, (1975).

Klaus, Patsy A. and Michael R. Rand. "Family Violence," Bureau of Justice Statistics, Special Report, U.S. Department of Justice, (April 1984): 1–5.

Korb, Dr. Lawrence, speech, Federal Women's Program Interagency Advisory Group Meeting (October 8, 1982).

————. speech, "Defense and the Employment of Spouses—A Military Retention Issue," Federal Women's Program Observance, Washington, D.C. (March 7, 1983). File Service No. 16, April 1983. Prepared by the Office of the Chief of Public Affairs, Department of the Army.

"Law Enforcement Role Vital to Family Advocacy Work," *Military Family*. (September–October 1986): 5.

Lee, Captain Daniel B., ACSW, Tripler Army Medical Center, Hawaii. "A Study on Global Phenomena of the U.S. Military Intermarriage: A New Interventional Dimension."

"Library Privileges for Spouses of Sponsors," Disposition Form, Maria Markusfeld, Community Librarian (May 10, 1983).

MacLennan, Beryce W. Ph.D. "Problems in Estimating the Nature and Extent of Family Violence in the Armed Forces," National Defense University, Washington, D.C. (April 1985).

Makowsky, Paula P., et. al. "Women's Perceived Stress and Well-Being Following Voluntary and Involuntary Relocation." Colorado State University, Human Development and Family Studies, Fort Collins, Colorado.

"Marriage Info Check Sheet," for service members wishing to marry Philippine citizens.

"Marriage in Oversea Commands," Army Regulation No. 600-240 (June 1, 1978).

"Marriage Procedures," Department of the Air Force, Hickam Air Force Base, Hawaii (August 14, 1986).

Marrott, Major Dwayne D., Division Psychologist. "An Assessment of the Needs of Foreign-Born Wives in the 25th Division, Schofield Barracks," Hawaii (1986).

Martin, James A., Ph.D., and Jeanette R. Ickovics. "Challenges of Military Life: The Importance of a Partnership Between the Army and Its Families," *Military Family* (November–December 1986) Vol. 6, No. 6: 3–5.

\*                                           \*                                           \*

Martin, Maj. James A., MSC. "The Military Wife," *Medical Bulletin of the US Army, Europe.* (January 1984) Vol. 41, No. 1): 12–18.

McCubbin, Hamilton I., Barbara B. Dahl, Gary R. Lester and Thomas Hammond. "Fathers at Sea: Characteristics of Navy Families Vulnerable to the Stresses of Separation." Paper, Family Studies Branch, Center for Prisoner of War Studies, Naval Health Research Center, San Diego, California.

McCullah, Robert D. "Effects of Family Dysfunction on Military Operations: Mental Health Needs," *The Military Family and the Military Organization* eds. Edna J. Hunter and Thomas C. Shaylor, Washington, D.C.: The Adjutant General Center (1978): 33.

McGuire, Mynda, ed. "Family Support Centers Aid Retention," *Family News*, (February 1986): 1–3.

McHugh, Ed. "Career Opportunities for Spouses of Military and Civilian Employees," U.S. Office of Personnel Management (December 1982/January 1983) Vol. 2, No. 4: 3.

"Men Opposed to Violent Encounter," Domestic Violence Prevention Center, Colorado Springs, Colorado.

Metcalf, Captain Merle, USN. "Is Love Enough to Make a Marriage?" Chaplain's Office, Subic Bay, Philippines.

*Military Family.* Vol. 7, No. 1 (January–February 1987).

*Military Family*, "Family Resources," undated.

"Military Family Act," Official Bulletin for Army Civilian Employees in Hawaii (November 1986), 3–5.

"Military Family Resource Center (MFRC) Completes Jurisdictional Study," *Military Family*, (May–June 1986): 6: 3, 1–4.

"Military Spouse and Family Issues," Europe 1982, National Military Families Association, Washington, D.C.

Momiyama, Lieutenant Colonel Augustine T., ACSW. Tripler Army Medical Center, "Social and Clinical Observations of American Servicemen and Their Foreign-Born Spouses."

National Military Family Association brochure.

Navy Family Service Center, Personal Assistance Center February 1986 Programs.

Neidig, Peter H. "Domestic Violence in the Military," Part I, II, *Military Family* (July–August 1985): 3–5.

NiCarthy, Ginny, Karen Merrian and Sandra Coffman. "Talking It Out," a brainwashing, coercion chart.

**217**

O'Beirne, Kathleen P. "Waiting Wives." *United States Naval Institute Proceedings*, (September 1976): 28, 30–37.

———. "While the Husband's Away." *Wifeline*, (Fall 1976): 1, 8.

"Off-Post Housing," Army Regulations, AR210-50, Section VII (February 1, 1982).

"Parenting Solo in the Service," AT&T's Military Lifeguide.

Pedersen, Paul B., Ph.D. "Ten Frequent Assumptions of Cultural Bias in Counseling." *Military Family*, (January–February 1987): 3–5.

"Programs for Aliamanu Residents," Aliamanu Military Reservation, Armed Services YMCA, Hawaii.

"Promoting Family Wellness," handout. Family Stress and Coping Project, Family Social Science, University of Minnesota.

Reenlistment Studies, Department of the Navy (April 23, 1979).

Reilly, Philip J. "The Korean Character and Cross Cultural Marriage."

"Rights and Benefits." *Wifeline*, (Spring 1987).

Russell, Christine. "Family Violence in Military," Walter Reed Army Institute of Research, 197-200.

Ross, Gary J. "Getting a job: You have an edge," *Wifeline*, (Winter 1988): 4.

"SecDef Underscores Importance of Family Advocacy Programs," *Military Family*, (September–October 1986): 1.

"Services Assisting Family Environments" (SAFE), Col. Mayo K. Ellingson, MSC, USA, Kenneth Lee, MSW.

"Service Delivery Assessment Report on Domestic Violence." Inspector General's Report. Department of Health, Education and Welfare, (August 31, 1979). (Cited by Bok-Lim C. Kim, 52–53.)

"Services Helping the Service," AT&T's Military Lifeguide, #4.

Snyder, Alice Ivey. "Separations and Reunions: Their Impact on the Submariner's Wife," Doctoral Dissertation, University of Hawaii, (May 1979).

———. "Sea and Shore Rotation: The Family and Separation," Office of Naval Research, Department of the Navy, (October 1, 1977).

———. "Separations and Sexuality: The Navy Case," Paper, (January 24, 1981).

"Sole Parents," *Commanders Call* (March–April 1979): 2–5.

"Sole Parents," Department of Defense Report, October 1981.

Sonkin, Daniel Jay, Ph.D. "The Male Batterer: An Overview (Part II)", *Military Family*. (March–April 1985): 5: 2, 9-1.

"Spouse Abuse Treatment Program Reference," Academy of Health Sciences, U.S. Army, GR 51-240-089.

★                              ★                              ★

"Spouse Abuse Within the Armed Forces on Okinawa," an unpublished report, U.S.A.F., (1986).

"Spouse Issues Blue Ribbon Panel Report" (March 1988) United States Air Force.

Spouse Needs Assessment, Department of the Air Force, Family Action and Information Board.

"Spouse Preference Under the Military Family Act of 1985," Department of the Army, Washington, D.C. (September 29, 1986).

"Spouse Abuse Within the Armed Forces on Okinawa."

"Spring Clean-up, Bldg. 1007," Disposition Form, MSG Everett J. Hennie, Vogelweh Military Housing Area, Germany, (May 7, 1983).

"Survey of Working Women," conducted by the Federal Women's Programs, Kaiserlautern, West Germany, (1982).

"Toughest Job in the Navy." *Wifeline*, (Winter 1987): 1–3.

Trost, Admiral Carlisle A. H. "Spouse Employment." *Wifeline*, (Spring 1987): 2.

Watts, Vivian E. "Basic Facts on Women in the Work Force."

Welch, Gen. Larry D. and E. C. Aldridge, Jr. "Air Force Blue Ribbon Panel Report Spouse Issues."

"Wellness in the Home," Services Assisting Family Environments, Camp H. M. Smith, Hawaii.

World War II Depository Records, University of Hawaii, Hamilton Library, Hawaiian/Pacific Room.

*Television Reports*

Ross, Brian. "NBC Nightly News": "Korean Slave Trade," June 27, 1988. "G.I.'s and Prostitutes," June 28, 1988.

# AIR FORCE TIMES PAY CHART

New monthly basic pay effective Jan. 1, 1990

## Commissioned officers

| Grade | Less than 2 | 2 | 3 | 4 | 6 | 8 | 10 | 12 | 14 | 16 | 18 | 20 | 22 | 26 |
|---|---|---|---|---|---|---|---|---|---|---|---|---|---|---|
| O-10 | 5710.80 | 5911.80 | 5911.80 | 5911.80 | 5911.80 | 6291.60 | 6291.60 | 6291.60 | 6291.60 | 6291.60 | 6291.60 | 6291.60 | 6291.60 | 6291.60 |
| O-9 | 5061.30 | 5193.90 | 5304.30 | 5304.30 | 5304.30 | 5439.30 | 5439.30 | 5665.80 | 5665.80 | 6291.60 | 6291.60 | 6291.60 | 6291.60 | 6291.60 |
| O-8 | 4584.30 | 4721.40 | 4833.60 | 4833.60 | 4833.60 | 5193.90 | 5193.90 | 5439.30 | 5439.30 | 5665.80 | 5911.80 | 6291.60 | 6291.60 | 6291.60 |
| O-7 | 3809.10 | 4068.80 | 4068.80 | 4068.80 | 4250.40 | 4250.40 | 4496.70 | 4496.70 | 4721.40 | 5193.90 | 5911.80 | 5911.80 | 6291.60 | 6291.60 |
| O-6 | 2823.30 | 3102.00 | 3305.10 | 3305.10 | 3305.10 | 3305.10 | 3305.10 | 3305.10 | 3417.30 | 3957.90 | 4159.80 | 4250.40 | 4496.70 | 5551.20 |
| O-5 | 2257.80 | 2651.40 | 2834.70 | 2834.70 | 2834.70 | 2834.70 | 2920.50 | 3077.40 | 3288.30 | 3529.50 | 3732.00 | 3845.10 | 3979.20 | 4877.10 |
| O-4 | 1903.50 | 2317.80 | 2472.30 | 2472.30 | 2518.20 | 2629.20 | 2808.60 | 2966.40 | 3102.00 | 3237.90 | 3327.60 | 3327.60 | 3327.60 | 3327.60 |
| O-3 | 1768.80 | 1977.60 | 2114.10 | 2339.10 | 2451.00 | 2538.90 | 2676.30 | 2808.60 | 2877.90 | 2877.90 | 2877.90 | 2877.90 | 2877.90 | 2877.90 |
| O-2 | 1542.30 | 1684.50 | 2023.50 | 2091.60 | 2135.40 | 2135.40 | 2135.40 | 2135.40 | 2135.40 | 2135.40 | 2135.40 | 2135.40 | 2135.40 | 2135.40 |
| O-1 | 1338.90 | 1394.10 | 1684.50 | 1684.50 | 1684.50 | 1684.50 | 1684.50 | 1684.50 | 1684.50 | 1684.50 | 1684.50 | 1684.50 | 1684.50 | 1684.50 |

## Officers with more than 4 years active duty as enlisted or warrant officer

| Grade | Less than 2 | 2 | 3 | 4 | 6 | 8 | 10 | 12 | 14 | 16 | 18 | 20 | 22 | 26 |
|---|---|---|---|---|---|---|---|---|---|---|---|---|---|---|
| O-3E | 0.00 | 0.00 | 0.00 | 0.00 | 2451.00 | 2538.90 | 2676.30 | 2808.60 | 2920.50 | 2920.50 | 2920.50 | 2920.50 | 2920.50 | 2920.50 |
| O-2E | 0.00 | 0.00 | 0.00 | 0.00 | 2135.40 | 2202.90 | 2317.80 | 2406.30 | 2472.30 | 2472.30 | 2472.30 | 2472.30 | 2472.30 | 2472.30 |
| O-1E | 0.00 | 0.00 | 0.00 | 1684.50 | 1799.40 | 1865.70 | 1933.20 | 2000.70 | 2091.60 | 2091.60 | 2091.60 | 2091.60 | 2091.60 | 2091.60 |

## Enlisted members

| Grade | Less than 2 | 2 | 3 | 4 | 6 | 8 | 10 | 12 | 14 | 16 | 18 | 20 | 22 | 26 |
|---|---|---|---|---|---|---|---|---|---|---|---|---|---|---|
| E-9 | 0.00 | 0.00 | 0.00 | 0.00 | 0.00 | 0.00 | 2096.10 | 2143.50 | 2192.10 | 2242.20 | 2292.30 | 2337.00 | 2459.70 | 2694.80 |
| E-8 | 0.00 | 0.00 | 0.00 | 0.00 | 0.00 | 1758.00 | 1808.10 | 1855.80 | 1904.10 | 1954.20 | 1999.20 | 2048.40 | 2168.70 | 2410.20 |
| E-7 | 1227.30 | 1324.80 | 1374.00 | 1422.00 | 1470.60 | 1517.40 | 1566.00 | 1614.60 | 1687.80 | 1735.80 | 1784.70 | 1807.20 | 1928.70 | 2168.70 |
| E-6 | 1056.00 | 1150.80 | 1198.80 | 1249.80 | 1296.30 | 1343.40 | 1392.90 | 1464.60 | 1510.50 | 1559.40 | 1583.10 | 1583.10 | 1583.10 | 1583.10 |
| E-5 | 926.70 | 1008.60 | 1057.50 | 1103.70 | 1176.00 | 1224.00 | 1272.60 | 1319.00 | 1343.40 | 1343.40 | 1343.40 | 1343.40 | 1343.40 | 1343.40 |
| E-4 | 864.30 | 912.60 | 966.30 | 1041.30 | 1082.40 | 1082.40 | 1082.40 | 1082.40 | 1082.40 | 1082.40 | 1082.40 | 1082.40 | 1082.40 | 1082.40 |
| E-3 | 814.20 | 858.90 | 893.40 | 928.80 | 928.80 | 928.80 | 928.80 | 928.80 | 928.80 | 928.80 | 928.80 | 928.80 | 928.80 | 928.80 |
| E-2 | 783.60 | 783.60 | 783.60 | 783.60 | 783.60 | 783.60 | 783.60 | 783.60 | 783.60 | 783.60 | 783.60 | 783.60 | 783.60 | 783.60 |
| E-1 | 699.00 | 699.00 | 699.00 | 699.00 | 699.00 | 699.00 | 699.00 | 699.00 | 699.00 | 699.00 | 699.00 | 699.00 | 699.00 | 699.00 |

E-1 with less than 4 months—646.20

## Basic allowance for quarters

| Pay grade | Without Full | Without Partial | With |
|---|---|---|---|
| O-10 | 613.20 | 50.70 | 754.50 |
| O-9 | 613.20 | 50.70 | 754.50 |
| O-8 | 613.20 | 50.70 | 754.50 |
| O-7 | 613.20 | 50.70 | 754.50 |
| O-6 | 562.50 | 39.60 | 679.80 |
| O-5 | 541.80 | 33.00 | 654.00 |
| O-4 | 502.20 | 26.70 | 577.80 |
| O-3 | 402.60 | 22.20 | 478.20 |
| O-2 | 319.50 | 17.70 | 408.00 |
| O-1 | 268.80 | 13.20 | 364.50 |
| O-3E | 434.40 | 22.20 | 513.30 |
| O-2E | 369.60 | 17.70 | 463.20 |
| O-1E | 317.70 | 13.20 | 428.10 |
| E-9 | 372.00 | 18.60 | 490.50 |
| E-8 | 342.00 | 15.30 | 452.10 |
| E-7 | 291.90 | 12.00 | 420.30 |
| E-6 | 264.00 | 9.90 | 387.90 |
| E-5 | 243.60 | 8.70 | 348.90 |
| E-4 | 212.10 | 8.10 | 303.60 |
| E-3 | 208.20 | 7.80 | 282.30 |
| E-2 | 169.20 | 7.20 | 268.80 |
| E-1 | 150.30 | 6.90 | 268.80 |

## Basic allowance for subsistence

Officers (including commissioned officers, warrants and aviation cadets): $119.61 per month

| Enlisted | 4 mos. | Others |
|---|---|---|
| Rations in kind not available | $5.95 | $6.44 |
| On leave or granted permission to mess separately | 5.27 | 5.70 |
| Emergency conditions where no government messing is available | 7.59 | 8.53 |

Source: DoD Compensation Office

ATPCC

# Index

**223**